SELF-LOVE WORKBOOK FOR WOMEN— TRAUMA RECOVERY

SELF-LOVE WORKBOOK FOR WOMEN–

TRAUMA RECOVERY

Empowering Exercises to Build Self-Worth, Self-Care, and Self-Trust

JORDAN BROWN, LPC

callisto
publishing
an imprint of Sourcebooks

This Workbook
Belongs To:

CONTENTS

INTRODUCTION

Healing trauma is a gift you're giving yourself—a beautiful, challenging, and rewarding gift. It's life-changing, and sometimes even lifesaving, to embrace self-care and release yourself from the hurtful experiences and painful memories of the past.

Processing and recovering from trauma, whether the traumatic experiences are more recent or further in the past, is a complicated and difficult journey for everyone. But the same experience can have a completely different impact on the lives of different people. An experience that was traumatic for you may not have been for another person, and vice versa. We all have different reactions to trauma and different ways of processing it and healing, and that's completely normal.

I'm honored to be here with you, as I have walked, and continue to walk, the trauma healing journey myself. The effects of trauma have shown up in many different ways in my life: people-pleasing, perfectionism, unhealthy coping skills, repressed memories, avoidance behaviors, and a deep desire for connection with people who will accept me for me. Through my journey so far, I've cultivated a strong sense of self-worth and self-love, and learned to set the boundaries I need, embrace my imperfections, confront challenges head-on, and hold space for meaningful, life-enhancing relationships.

As a licensed professional counselor for the past ten years, specializing in working with women who are experiencing low self-worth and anxiety, most often as a result of trauma, I love helping my clients recover. Experiencing and witnessing the hurtful impacts of trauma,

as well as the transformative power of healing, motivated me to write this workbook to reach more people, such as you. We all deserve to heal from the hurts of our past and move toward a brighter and more hopeful future.

This book will offer you a relatable, practical, and strength-based lens to guide you toward healing. While a workbook is a great way to help you better understand trauma and work through the range of complicated feelings it brings up, it is not a replacement for medical treatment or working with a mental health professional. Please know that there is no shame in reaching out for help or seeking treatment.

The book includes anecdotes of individuals who have experienced trauma. These stories are based on actual clinical experience with clients; however, the people described are not real individuals but rather reflect composites of several similar clients.

As a trauma survivor, you are not broken. You have been hurt and are carrying a wound. By choosing to use this workbook, you have already taken a courageous step in the direction of healing. I see you and your efforts in showing up here. Whether you are just starting to explore ways to heal or are months or years in, I am so grateful to be walking alongside you for this part of your journey.

HOW TO USE THIS BOOK

You'll find two main sections in this workbook. Part 1 is foundational information on trauma, while part 2 is filled with practical exercises and tools for processing, managing, and healing trauma.

You may choose to go through this workbook from start to finish, or you can flip to specific sections, depending on what you need in the moment. If you feel you could benefit from more information on trauma or if you're newer to trauma healing, I suggest starting with part 1 to lay a solid base for the rest of your work throughout the book.

Although I recommend using this book together with a therapist, it can be used on your own. Therapists may use this workbook to guide or supplement their sessions or recommend it as homework for clients to do between sessions.

Due to the nature of trauma and healing, I encourage you to take things slowly and pay attention to how you feel as you begin this workbook. If you start to feel overwhelmed or distressed or notice any increase in symptoms of depression or anxiety, please have patience with yourself and strongly consider taking a break or working through the rest of the book with a therapist. The Resources section on page 169 has more information on finding help.

Trauma healing is a slow, ongoing process of learning and relearning about yourself, others, and the world around you. It's okay if you can't commit to working through this book consistently. Take it at your own pace, and focus on doing what you can and learning what you need.

PART I

The Truth About Trauma

When it comes to healing, knowledge is power. Trauma can make it difficult to trust, and that leads to uncertainty, anxiety, and fear. Gaining knowledge can help ease the discomfort of uncertainty, calm your nervous system, and lead you forward on your healing path with more confidence.

In part 1, you will find many helpful nuggets of knowledge to help you explore the legacy of trauma in your own life. The goal is to better understand trauma and your responses to it, feel empowered in your resilience, and prepare for healing by exploring tips for establishing safety, remembering your strengths, facing challenges, and embracing change as you start your journey.

HOW TRAUMA SHOWS UP

Trauma can show up in many different ways—in some ways you might be aware of and in others that might surprise you. It can show up internally by affecting how you think and feel, and it can show up externally by affecting your behaviors and how you interact and connect with others. You may not yet realize all the ways trauma shows up for you. That's okay. This section, as well as the information and exercises you'll find throughout the rest of this book, will give you more insight into how it shows up for you.

In this section, you'll also discover what trauma is, how it can affect women differently, and common myths about trauma. You'll find lots of validation, compassion, and encouragement, as well. As a trauma survivor, it can be hard to embrace your strengths or see yourself in a positive light. Until you're ready to do that for yourself, I'm happy to be your guide out of the darkness and toward the light that I hope you will find on your journey of recovery.

I'm so glad you survived what you've been through, and I'm proud of you for being here to take the next steps toward healing.

> "Trauma is not what happens to you, but what happens inside you as a result of what happens to you."
> —GABOR MATÉ

Heather's Story: Healing Her Sense of Self

Heather, the oldest child of nine siblings, grew up in a mixed-race family where many of the older family members carried their own unresolved trauma. This affected Heather and the family as a whole. She experienced a series of early traumatic experiences, including parentification (when a child has to take care of a parent or take on the responsibilities of being a parent), parental rejection, and racism. When Heather was a teenager, she chose to come out to her family as bisexual. Unfortunately, her family was not accepting or supportive. This trauma intensified many of the feelings Heather had already been experiencing of identity confusion and *I'm not good enough* and *Something must be wrong with me*.

Heather's well-being was deeply compromised. She became shut off from her emotions and struggled in relationships with family, friends, and romantic partners. She felt shame about who she was and had trouble taking care of herself, often putting others' needs before her own.

Eventually, a trusted family member suggested Heather go to therapy. Through individual and group therapy, Heather has started to chip away at the belief there was something wrong with her, empowering her to make healthier choices for her self-care and in her relationships.

WHAT IS TRAUMA?

Trauma is more than a traumatic event. It includes the biological and protective responses your mind and body develop as a result of experiences that happen too fast, too much, or too soon in life—or not enough (like neglect)—for your nervous system to handle. These experiences most often involve a situation in which your mental, emotional, or physical well-being is in danger, and they overwhelm your ability to cope.

The initial biological response to trauma jump-starts your internal threat defense system: fight, flight, freeze, or fawn (try to appease). If the trauma remains unresolved or you experience repeated trauma, your mind and body adapt to cope with the ongoing stress by creating longer-term protective and defensive responses, such as holding tension in your body, escaping through substance use, shutting down emotionally, and people-pleasing, to name a few.

While it may not seem like it, these responses were actually necessary to help you survive the traumatic event(s). But when they stick around after you are no longer in immediate danger, they become unhelpful or even counterproductive. You no longer need this kind of protection, and these continued protective responses can keep you stuck in unhelpful patterns and unresolved trauma.

Post-traumatic stress disorder (PTSD) can develop after experiencing a single traumatic event, such as a car accident. Complex post-traumatic stress disorder (C-PSTD, or complex trauma) results from repeated traumatic events, which often, but not always, involve childhood or relational traumas (traumas stemming from personal or social relationships), such as chronic bullying.

Many different experiences can cause trauma. Some are easily identifiable, such as abuse or living in a war zone; others may be harder to recognize, such as emotional neglect or growing up with parents or siblings who were struggling with their mental health. Try not to compare your experiences to anyone else's. If you have developed emotional or physical protective responses (sometimes called *mind-body adaptations*) as a result of dangerous, painful, or harmful events in your life, your experiences and your responses to them are valid for you.

WHAT TRAUMA LOOKS LIKE

There are some common trauma responses (that is, mind-body symptoms and your protective responses) you may experience, although these common trauma responses can look different for each person. Each response has a range of ways it can manifest, and each can vary in how severe it is and how it affects your life. Here are five of the most common trauma responses.

Feelings of Shame: Experiencing trauma often creates inaccurate and distorted narratives about yourself and others. This can lead to the belief that you are to blame for the trauma you experienced or that there is something wrong with you for having had the experience. Taking on shame and blame is a response that helps you make sense of a situation that otherwise feels overwhelmingly senseless.

Difficulty with Emotions: You may go back and forth between feeling overwhelmed by your emotions and avoiding or numbing them. This difficulty with managing your emotions and your reactions to them is called *emotional dysregulation*. This is a common trauma response because of the way trauma alters or impairs (dysregulates) the nervous system. Your brain then sends out signals to either overreact or underreact to protect you, even when you no longer need protection. This dysregulation can take the form of panic or unhealthy rage, or the opposite, feeling numb or withdrawn.

Hypervigilance: One way animals survive in the wild is by remaining on high alert to any changes in their environment that might signal danger. After you experience a traumatic event, you may feel something similar. Your internal alarm system becomes heightened and easily triggered, leaving you feeling jumpy or easily startled, and this can continue even after the threat of danger has passed. This is called *hypervigilance*; it's being on guard and on high alert to your surroundings in an effort to keep yourself safe.

Unhealthy Coping Strategies: Trauma survivors often develop unhealthy coping strategies because they do not have a lot of healthy resources to help manage the overwhelming emotions and memories of traumatic events. This is especially true for survivors of childhood trauma. Some common unhealthy coping strategies are substance misuse and addictions, eating disorders, and self-harm. While it may seem counterintuitive, on some level these behaviors are an attempt to survive the emotional distress of trauma and regulate the nervous system. If you are struggling with these issues, there are resources on page 169 that will point you to finding more help.

Relationship Issues: Trauma, especially relational trauma that happens within a close relationship, can deeply affect your ability to create and maintain healthy relationships. You may find yourself repeating cycles of unhealthy relationships, struggling with interpersonal skills, or unintentionally sabotaging healthy relationships. As with feelings of shame, the inaccurate and distorted views of yourself and others that can result from trauma can make it difficult to recognize, navigate, and maintain healthy relationships.

WOMEN AND TRAUMA

While trauma can affect anyone, there is evidence that women may be especially affected by its impact. Of course, just as the experience of women varies across age, race, culture, and many other factors, the impact of trauma among women varies, too. However, evidence still points toward numerous reasons that women tend to experience a greater impact from traumatic experiences than others.

Women are more likely than men to experience trauma earlier in life, and are also more likely to experience traumatic events such as sexual abuse and physical and sexual violence by an intimate partner. This kind of trauma tends to lead to more severe and longer-lasting effects.

Women may also feel less safe doing things that men don't necessarily view as unsafe, such as walking down the street or shopping alone. This can leave them with a fearful view of the world and the people around them, and they may become hypervigilant. Feeling unsafe, whether the threat is real or perceived, can make a person more likely to experience trauma, and it can make responses from other traumatic events worse.

Women who live in cultures that hold traditional gender roles are more at risk for experiencing the effects of trauma, because they feel more emotionally vulnerable and may lack strong support systems.

As women, we may be at greater risk of being affected by trauma, but we are also incredibly strong and resilient. We do not have control over everything that happens to us and around us or the ways in which society continues to create traumatic environments. But we can choose to make changes in our own little corner of the world by healing our trauma, not passing it on to future generations, and showing others that it's possible to find a brighter future.

COMMON TRAUMA SYMPTOMS

To help you get a sense of your current trauma responses, take a moment to reflect on whether you're currently experiencing any of these common responses. Read each statement and then circle whether you experience the trauma response never, sometimes, or often. Remember, there is nothing wrong with you if you experience these trauma responses; they are signs that you are a warrior with a strong will to survive.

1. **I have difficulty concentrating.**
   Never / Sometimes / Often

2. **I struggle to manage my emotions.**
   Never / Sometimes / Often

3. I have trouble trusting myself and others.
   Never / Sometimes / Often

4. I feel tense or on edge and have difficulty relaxing.
   Never / Sometimes / Often

5. I feel disconnected from myself or the world around me.
   Never / Sometimes / Often

6. I tend to avoid my difficult thoughts, memories, or emotions.
   Never / Sometimes / Often

7. I use unhealthy coping skills to deal with what I've experienced.
   Never / Sometimes / Often

8. I feel like I am not enough or like there is something wrong with me.
   Never / Sometimes / Often

9. I feel isolated or detached from others, including my family and friends.
   Never / Sometimes / Often

10. I have difficulty with sleep or feel exhausted even after a full night of sleep.
    Never / Sometimes / Often

11. I blame myself for my mistakes, shortcomings, and the unwanted experiences I've had.
    Never / Sometimes / Often

12. I have nightmares, flashbacks, or unwanted memories that seem to come out of nowhere.
    Never / Sometimes / Often

Remember, trauma can look different for everyone. Take some time to reflect on your answers. Then ask yourself:

- Which trauma response currently has the most impact on my life?
- How has this trauma response protected me or helped me survive?

As you read this book, you'll find a variety of skills and resources to help manage your symptoms.

This checklist is meant for self-reflection; it is not an official diagnostic tool. Some symptoms on this list can be related to other mental health conditions that can occur together with trauma, such as depression, anxiety, attention-deficit/hyperactivity disorder (ADHD), and others. Exploring your symptoms with a therapist can help you better understand and support yourself on your healing journey.

TIPS FOR WHEN YOU FEEL OVERWHELMED

When you're reading or thinking about trauma, you may start to feel overwhelmed. Practicing mindfulness—very intentionally being aware of your thoughts, emotions, body sensations, and surroundings without judgment—is a great way to bring yourself to the present moment and help ease feelings of being overwhelmed and stressed. Here are three simple mindfulness exercises you can use whenever you need them:

Slow, Rhythmic Breathing (4-7-8): Breathing exercises help by calming your nervous system, allowing you to think more clearly, improving your mood, and reducing stress. For this practice, sit in a comfortable position, inhale for four seconds, hold for seven seconds, and exhale for eight seconds. Count slowly and at an even pace, and repeat this pattern for five minutes to start. You can gradually add more time as you use this exercise. (Breathing exercises can be challenging for some trauma survivors, who may feel uneasy focusing on their bodily sensations. If you notice this happening, try incorporating breathwork very slowly. Meanwhile, use other resources that have less focus on breathing, such as the grounding technique on this list, or consult with a therapist.)

Mindful Movement: Mindful movement helps you feel calmer in the present moment by focusing on your breath and how your body feels as it moves. You can do this with any type of movement you enjoy, such as walking, stretching, yoga, or dancing. For example, you might take a short walk and pay close attention to how the ground feels under your feet and how your breath moves through your body.

Grounding in the Present Moment: Grounding techniques are excellent tools to help you refocus on the present moment. This draws you away from past or distressing thoughts, emotions, and memories. Most grounding techniques involve your senses. For this practice, pause and notice your surroundings. What do you see, hear, smell, feel, and (if applicable) taste? You can also add a grounding statement such as *I'm safe here*. Continue noticing your surroundings and repeating your grounding statement until you feel calmer.

MYTHS ABOUT TRAUMA

As with most topics in mental health, we continue to learn more about trauma all the time. In fact, PTSD was first recognized as a mental health diagnosis only in 1980, and C-PTSD, or complex trauma, is even newer than that. (Complex trauma has yet to be recognized as an official diagnosis by the American Psychiatric Association, but efforts are being made to change this.) Therefore, there are still some common misunderstandings and myths about trauma.

Unfortunately, some people in your life may say things that minimize, judge, or dismiss your experience. They may judge you because they do not understand the trauma responses you are experiencing and all the ways they can impact your life. Or they may be stuck in the idea that trauma can only look a certain way. No matter who they are or what they say, remember that your experience and your feelings are real and valid.

- **Myth 1: Only events such as seeing combat in war or experiencing physical abuse can cause trauma.** Trauma can be the result of a wide range of experiences, from war combat and violent crime to discrimination and emotional neglect.

- **Myth 2: Trauma is just made up in your mind.** Trauma is very real. The mind-body responses and symptoms and their impact on people's lives tell us so. Brain scans can even show us the effects of trauma on the brain.

- **Myth 3: You should be able to easily move on from a traumatic event or events.** Because of the deeply impactful changes that happen, simply moving on from trauma is usually not possible. Rather, trauma involves a slow recovery process to heal the mind and body.

- **Myth 4: Everyone who experiences trauma gets PTSD or C-PTSD.** You can experience trauma symptoms and develop mind-body responses without meeting the criteria for PTSD or C-PTSD. For example, you might have difficulty sleeping and feel on edge after being in a serious car accident, but not meet the other criteria for a PTSD diagnosis.

- **Myth 5: Trauma will have a negative impact on your life forever**. Trauma changes your mind and body in adaptive survival ways. Healing changes your mind and body by moving you out of survival mode and into states of calm, connection, and joy. In fact, you can eventually reach post-traumatic growth, in which the positive changes you experience as you heal help you find an even better life than the one you had before your trauma. Although this doesn't mean the impact of trauma on your life will completely go away (it might for some people and won't for others), the degree of impact can change and lessen over the course of your healing journey as you learn to get ahead of and manage symptoms. You absolutely can have a joyful, connected, and meaningful life.

Your Resilience

Simply by being here today and having made it through the event(s) you've experienced, you have already demonstrated remarkable resilience. You have successfully adapted to and survived difficult and challenging circumstances. Take a moment to reflect on the positive qualities you possess, such as courage, persistence, determination, and hope for something different and better.

When approaching your healing journey, remembering to acknowledge and appreciate your strengths will help you continue to embody resilience. Understanding trauma as mind-body responses that helped you survive and kept you safe is a strength-based way to ease shame and self-judgment and to foster self-compassion and resilience in healing. You are not wrong or bad for having the responses you've had; you are a strong survivor.

No matter where you are on your healing journey, at times you may feel less resilient or less optimistic about yourself and the healing process. That's okay. A common trauma response is negative thinking patterns, and as humans, we are already wired with a bias for focusing on negativity. If you find yourself there, try to:

- **Use self-compassion to bring yourself to the present moment.** Trauma tries to pull you into the past.
- **Remind yourself you are not alone.** Many people out there have moments of doubt on their healing journeys, too.
- **Give yourself some compassionate self-talk.** Be the support you need.

HEALING IS POSSIBLE

Recovery from trauma is possible. It may not feel like it at times, but I can assure you that it is. I've seen it time and again with my clients, and I've experienced it on my own personal healing journey. Recovery is possible because our nervous systems are wired for healing. Our job is to give our minds and bodies the support, safety, and care they need and to trust our nervous systems to do what they're meant to do: heal.

Trauma recovery is a beautiful, challenging, and ongoing journey. Trauma happens when an experience overwhelms your nervous system, and you can't heal when you're overwhelmed. This is why trauma healing happens slowly, allowing you time and space to increase your tolerance and build healthy resources to manage overwhelming thoughts and emotions.

You may have felt alone when you experienced trauma, but you do not need to heal alone. In fact, support is an essential part of healing. And not just any support, but help that consists of people and places that are safe, trustworthy, and truly encouraging of your journey, such as a therapist and a stable living environment. The resources on page 169 will help you discover where to find additional support.

Congratulations on taking this important step on your healing journey. When the journey feels tough, or even impossible some days, remember that every step you take counts. No matter how small it may seem, it's progress toward the life you desire.

I am worthy and capable of this healing journey.

KEY TAKEAWAYS

Understanding what trauma is and how it can affect you sets a strong foundation for the next steps on your healing journey. Remember, trauma is not the event itself, but rather the emotional and physical protective responses you experience as a result of a traumatic event. The healing journey is meant to be done slowly and with support from safe and trusted others, such as a therapist or community support, and from yourself in the form of self-compassion and embracing your resilience. Healing is possible, and you've already taken positive steps on your journey by reading this section of the book.

- Your mind and body develop trauma responses as a result of experiences that happen too fast, too much, or too soon (or not enough) in life for your nervous system to handle.

- The initial fight/flight/freeze/fawn responses and longer-term protective and defensive responses were necessary to help you survive the traumatic event(s).

- Some common trauma responses include feelings of shame, difficulty with emotions, hypervigilance, unhealthy coping skills, and relationship issues.

- As women, we may be especially affected by trauma's impacts, but we are also incredibly strong and resilient.

- Trauma recovery is a beautiful, challenging, and ongoing journey.

PREPARING FOR YOUR HEALING JOURNEY

The motivation for starting your trauma recovery journey is different for everyone. Your motivation might be to improve your relationship with your partner, or maybe it's to heal so you don't pass along trauma to your children. Or maybe you can't shake chronic feelings of shame and sadness and find yourself isolating from others. My motivation to start healing was to alleviate my own suffering, improve my relationships with others, and help those around me, including my clients and anyone I encounter, which includes you and everyone else reading this book. Whatever your motivation for starting your healing journey, I'm so glad it brought you here.

Section 1 created a solid foundation for your healing journey, and section 2 will further solidify that foundation to help you feel more empowered and confident as you continue on. This section will walk you through starting where you're at, how to safely explore trauma, remembering your strengths, and embracing change. I'll offer practical tips for beginning your journey and what to do when you face challenges along the way (as everyone does).

I'm so excited for you to continue on your journey, and I hope you feel even better prepared for more learning, healing, and growth by the end of this section.

"Here's a theory: Maybe I had not really been broken this whole time. Maybe I had been a human—flawed and still growing but full of light nonetheless."

—STEPHANIE FOO

Lupe's Story: Taking One Step at a Time

Lupe came to therapy because she wanted to address the stress she was experiencing at work. She and her therapist built a strong, trusting relationship as they addressed her work stress and other issues in her life, including some traumatic events Lupe experienced as an adult. She was making progress but still was repeating unhealthy relationship patterns by choosing partners who were emotionally unavailable, not recognizing or ignoring red flags, and feeling as if she didn't deserve better.

Lupe was not able to fully engage in conversations about her family that were anything other than positive. She wasn't ready yet to process her childhood trauma and acknowledge her family had played a role in her current or past struggles. Her therapist recognized this, discussed it with Lupe, and was gentle and patient until Lupe felt ready.

Years into their work together, Lupe was ready to begin addressing the childhood trauma she experienced in her family. The foundation of her healthy attachment with her therapist, her healthy coping skills, and her supportive resources allowed Lupe to feel safe enough to finally look at the past that she had buried deep inside. While it has been an emotional and sometimes challenging journey, now that Lupe has been able to address her trauma and the delicate balance of maintaining relationships with her family, she has been able to make much more progress.

STARTING WHERE YOU'RE AT

As a therapist, it's important to meet my clients wherever they're at on their healing journeys, at whatever their current state of readiness for change. As you begin working through this book, it's just as important for you to meet yourself where you're at. This might mean skipping any parts you're not quite ready for, or reading through part 1 a few times before you feel ready to start the workbook activities in part 2.

While you meet yourself where you're at, remember to also show yourself compassion. No matter where you are on your journey, you're here. Some part of you feels ready to start or continue this healing journey. Give yourself credit for showing up for yourself by opening up this workbook and offer yourself kind, supportive, encouraging self-talk to keep going. If you get stuck, think about what you would say to a loved one who needs compassionate encouragement on their healing journey, and say the same thing to yourself.

REMEMBER YOUR STRENGTHS

Time and time again in my work with trauma survivors, I've been inspired by their incredible strength, even when they don't see it in themselves. I don't mean the old-fashioned idea of what it means to be strong, which is someone "tough" who suppresses their emotions, doesn't show their vulnerability, or learns to ignore pain. Instead, I'm referring to the life-enhancing skills that can support your survival through difficult life experiences.

We've already acknowledged your remarkable resilience and courage to make it this far on your journey and open this book. Perhaps you also have a fierce sense of fairness and call out wrongdoing when you see it in the world. You may be a loving and loyal friend or relative to the special people in your life. Maybe you are quick and resourceful in an emergency, or are known to have a great sense of humor, or are able to find gratitude in small pleasures in a way that most people overlook. However you define strength, I know you have plenty of it.

Remember, it's not the traumatic experiences that made you strong; you already had the strength you used to survive the adverse experience(s). Perhaps you adapted your strengths during or after those experiences, but they've been there in you all along.

Another thing to consider is that while unresolved trauma can be passed down from one generation to the next and the next, so can strength. Your ancestors survived their trauma. While they may not have gone through the healing process to resolve it, and therefore passed down trauma to you, they may have also passed down some of the strength and adaptive skills that allowed them to survive what they went through and helped you survive what you went through, as well.

If you're having trouble recognizing your strengths, consider how you define being strong. This doesn't mean ignoring the hurtful effects of the past, but instead defining strength on your own terms and allowing yourself to see it in you, because I know it's there.

SAFELY EXPLORING TRAUMA

Before we dive any deeper, let's talk about safety. Safety is the most important aspect of trauma healing. A traumatic experience has threatened your mental, emotional, and/or physical safety in some way, and you may have had difficulty feeling safe in your environment, your relationships, or your body since then. So establishing a foundation of safety is necessary for your healing process. It calms your nervous system and allows you to take an active approach to your healing from a place of choice, control, and empowerment.

It was very important to me to write this book with your safety and well-being in mind. It's also important for you to assess and reflect on your level of safety as you work through this book. If at any point you do not feel safe to continue, take a pause for as long as you need. This book will be here for you whenever you're ready to return to it.

The activities in this workbook will not ask you to recount painful memories, because that is best done with the assistance of a therapist. It's still likely that working through trauma will bring up difficult and painful thoughts, emotions, and memories, however. As a reminder, you can skip parts of the book as you wish and take breaks when you need to.

The many grounding and self-soothing practices included throughout this book are great resources to use if you begin to feel overwhelmed or distressed. Some good ones to start with include A Safe Container on page 54, Cultivating Connection in the Body on page 95, and Reclaiming Control and Choice on page 105.

TIPS FOR HEALING

Starting this journey can come with a wide range of emotions, from excitement to nervousness to feeling completely overwhelmed. Whatever you are feeling now is valid. Honor your excitement. Congratulate yourself for being nervous and doing this anyway. Acknowledge your overwhelmed feelings and remind yourself you will be okay.

Let's take a moment to soak in the gravity of what you're doing for yourself here. You've made it through so much, and you still chose to embark on this beautiful, challenging journey. The tips here offer guidance and suggestions for the path ahead.

Go at Your Own Pace

There is no timeline for healing; it looks different for everyone. It can take days, months, or even years to heal trauma, and it's often an ongoing process. That is, you'll continue to be an active participant in your healing by using your healthy coping skills and resources to take care of your mind and body into the future. Because most of my clients are living with the effects of trauma, and mostly complex trauma, we typically work together for years. During this time, we're able to form the strong, trusting relationship that survivors need, and we approach their trauma slowly and with great care. Part of that journey often includes assuring my clients they are not taking "too long" to heal. They are, in fact, making progress, and healing and making lasting changes take time.

Trauma healing is a complicated process that is not always linear and does not have a simple road map or formula to follow. Remember, whatever you are experiencing is a normal part of the process. Give yourself permission to go at your own pace through this book and throughout your healing journey.

Ride the Waves

When difficult thoughts and emotions come up, it may feel as if you're riding emotional waves. You can feel the distress gradually building and then decreasing. Your instinct may be to swim away from these waves with avoidance or distraction, but riding them to the top and over to the other side, allowing yourself to fully feel the depths of your difficult thoughts and emotions, is a necessary part of the journey from where you are now to a place of progress, growth, and healing. Slowly allow yourself to ride a wave for a longer period of time each time one comes. This gradual approach will help you ride the waves safely, reduce the sense of being overwhelmed, and build your ability to tolerate strong emotions.

The foundational aspects of part 1 will help you prepare to ride these waves. Part 2 provides you with tools and exercises to ride them. And I am here to ride these waves with you, too.

Put Yourself First

Putting yourself first is a common struggle for trauma survivors, as well as for women in general. Being able to do so is an important part of the trauma healing journey, because, as Arielle Schwartz says in

The Complex PTSD Workbook, it allows you "to respect your needs and feelings even when others do not." She adds that "a healthy form of selfishness is a key to well-being." Thinking of selfishness as always being bad is a kind of all-or-nothing thinking (thinking in extremes, without considering the possibilities that exist in the gray areas between those extremes). But you can think of selfishness as a spectrum from healthy to unhealthy. Reframing it this way can help you begin to prioritize yourself and your needs.

You might even create a PYF (Put Yourself First) routine, such as scheduling time for breaks, physical and mental self-care (such as personal hygiene, keeping a journal, and seeing a therapist), or just being alone. I suggest starting with one item in your PYF routine, and as you strengthen this habit, slowly adding other things. Allow for flexibility and protect the time you set aside for yourself.

Be Kind to Yourself

Self-love and self-compassion are key tools on your healing journey. When bad things happen to us, we tend to treat ourselves badly and shame and blame ourselves. Our internal threat defense system turns inward with self-criticism (fight), isolation (flight), ruminating thoughts (freeze), and hiding parts of ourselves from others (fawn). Self-compassion can be a healthier response by freeing us from distressing thoughts, emotions, and memories; reducing feelings of shame; and calming the nervous system.

Trauma can shatter your self-worth, and self-love can help rebuild that, or maybe help you develop healthy self-worth for the first time. Self-love and self-compassion can enhance emotional resilience, improve self-talk and self-care, and strengthen your relationships as you learn to set better boundaries. We'll approach these practices at a gentle pace throughout this workbook, so you can ease yourself into what may feel unfamiliar and uncomfortable at first.

Don't Be Afraid to Ask for Help

Trauma can make it difficult to trust others. Faced with circumstances you could not control, withholding trust may actually give you a sense of control, the feeling that you can protect yourself from harm, such as from rejection, abuse, and other mistreatment. You may have become highly independent and struggle to ask for help. When you don't ask for help, this can leave you feeling more isolated, lonely, disconnected, overwhelmed, overloaded, and feeling as if something is wrong with you.

Gently push yourself out of this zone of protection and into a zone of connection by seeking help from safe and trustworthy sources, such as a therapist, trusted family and friends, and community support, such as a support group, a recreational class or sport, or a spiritual community. These can be in person or online.

THERE ARE MANY PATHS TO HEALING

The truth is, there are many paths to healing. There is no one right way to recover and no wrong way to try.

As you explore part 2 of this workbook, you'll find many different tools and approaches you can use to help you heal. Some will ask you to write or create and others will ask you to move and get in touch with your body. It takes some experimenting with different tools and approaches to figure out what resonates and works best for you. While it can be difficult, don't compare yourself to others. Everyone has to take their own journey and find the unique path that works best for them.

No matter which path you take, there will be bumps along the way. Trauma recovery is not a smooth ride, and it doesn't need to be. When the bumps come, remind yourself this is a normal part of the process and the bumps don't mean you are doing something wrong. In fact, they mean you are doing something right.

For additional resources to explore as you continue your healing journey, see page 169.

HOW TO BEGIN YOUR JOURNEY

These practical tips will help you feel prepared and empowered as you gently begin this journey.

- **A safe environment is essential for your healing process.** Create a special place where you can feel comfortable and safe working through this book. This can be in your living environment, in a private area outside, or in a community space, such as a library. If you can, you might want to put comforting items, grounding objects, warm lighting, or fun decor in your special place.

- **Give yourself permission to bring your vulnerability.** It is very common for trauma survivors to shut off their vulnerability as a means of protection, but we need to be vulnerable in order to grow and heal. To be vulnerable, try to be as honest as you can, allow yourself to really feel the thoughts and emotions that come up, and approach the work with an open and curious mind.

- **Make a list of internal resources.** These are resources you can use when you feel overwhelmed or distressed during your healing journey. They might include grounding techniques, mindfulness practices, self-compassion exercises, and a healthy self-care routine. You can start creating your list with any resources you already have and add to it as you find other tools you like throughout this book.

- **Remember, be patient with yourself and your journey.** At times, you may feel immediate relief after using a tool or approach, and there will be other times when you don't notice the changes that are happening. Your mind-body responses exist on a spectrum. It will not be like a light switch, where trauma responses just go from completely on to completely off. There will be many steps along the way. Keep taking steps toward safety, presence, and connection by using the tools and approaches in this workbook at a pace that works for you.

- **Allow yourself to take missteps along the way.** *Perfectionism* (the tendency to place high, unrealistic standards of perfection on yourself to protect yourself from failure, criticism, rejection, and further trauma) is another common trauma response. It begins as a protective defense mechanism, but ultimately becomes unhelpful because it holds you back from stepping out of your comfort zone and meeting your goals. Perfectionism also keeps parts of yourself hidden (the parts you deem unworthy or feel ashamed of), which interferes with your ability to be vulnerable and develop deep connections with others and even yourself. Try to step out of any sense that you must be perfect and instead show up as your true, imperfect self. That will allow you to fully embrace the healing process.

CHALLENGES YOU MAY FACE

Sometimes the healing process feels worse before it starts to feel better, like riding the waves of difficult thoughts and emotions that come up during healing. This can feel discouraging, overwhelming, and uncomfortable—and it is a normal part of growth and change.

You may also feel like you don't have time to focus on your healing journey. I hear you; life can be busy, and it doesn't stop while you're working on healing. To dedicate time to your journey, try to schedule time to work through this book, whether that's once a day, once a week, or once a month, and also schedule time to use the tools and exercises in between. Remember that healing happens slowly, so knowing it may feel worse before it feels better, gradually riding more of each wave that comes, and working through this book in ways that work for you will help you feel safe as you make progress on your journey.

EMBRACING CHANGE

Have you ever gone back to a relationship you knew was unhealthy? Or continued to use coping skills that hurt you more than helped you? If you can relate, you're not alone. Our nervous system tends to find safety in what's familiar, even when it's not actually safe or helpful, until we teach it otherwise. When we are faced with familiar options, we can anticipate how to handle them, and that feels easier and less risky.

Because trauma can lead you to hold rigid, negative beliefs, your thinking can become fixed in the belief that you can't change and that who you are now is who you will always be. Gently trying new things and adopting positive thinking patterns can help you develop a growth mindset, which embraces setbacks as opportunities to learn and do better. This mindset has been shown to help lessen trauma symptoms and act as a foundation for post-traumatic growth.

When your nervous system finds safety in what's familiar, it can experience change as a threat. This may be why change has felt so scary and hard. Try to reframe change from scary and hard to opportunities for growth and necessary for healing. This will help you feel more open to and optimistic about change.

The good news is that you can teach your nervous system to recognize the familiar options and patterns that no longer serve you and to also recognize better but unfamiliar options as those that will bring you safety and peace. In part 2 of this book, you will find tools that can help you work toward retraining your nervous system.

KEY TAKEAWAYS

Trauma did not make you strong. Rather, you already had incredible strength that helped you survive what you went through. As you start and continue on your journey, remember to go at your own pace, ride the emotional waves, put yourself first, be kind to yourself, and don't be afraid to ask for help. Everyone's healing journey looks different, and yours is unique to you, but various practical tips and insights can help you feel more prepared, confident, and empowered as you start your healing journey and face challenges along the way.

- Give yourself credit for showing up for yourself by opening up this workbook, and offer yourself kind and supportive self-talk as encouragement to keep going.

- Establishing a foundation of safety calms your nervous system and allows you to take an active approach to your healing from a place of choice, control, and empowerment.

- The path of trauma healing comes in many forms; there is no one right way to recover. The best path is the one that feels right for you.

- You can retrain your nervous system to prefer safe but unfamiliar options to the familiar options and patterns that no longer serve you.

PART II

The Path to Healing

Welcome to part 2 of this book! Each section will offer exercises, strategies, practices, and affirmations to help you explore the legacy of trauma in your life and how you can begin to recover. To help you heal your mind, body, and soul and find your authentic wholeness, I've pulled from cognitive (thought-based), somatic (body-based), and experiential (experience-based) techniques and ideas.

I encourage you to try all the exercises slowly and with an open and curious mind. You will find that some are really helpful and others may not be. Some may be useful now, while others may be helpful when you revisit them in the future. It's all okay! My hope is that you'll walk away with new awareness and tools you can use to continue your healing journey and (re)claim self-love and joy in your life.

SECTION 3
LETTING GO OF SHAME

Healthy shame teaches us our limits and helps us learn from our mistakes. Toxic shame, which is what we're focusing on here, is the feeling that there is something wrong with or bad about you. Not that you did something wrong, but that *you* are wrong. Feeling shame is a hallmark of trauma because the messages, experiences, and unmet needs often related to trauma cause you to internalize feelings of shame, criticism, and unworthiness. Ironically, shame gives you a sense of control in situations where you would otherwise feel power-less, overwhelmed, and confused. I want you to know, and to eventually believe if you don't already, that **what happened to you was not your fault**.

With the shame you've felt, you may have buried, ignored, or abandoned parts of yourself, likely the most vulnerable and tender parts. In this section, I'll ask you to gently open yourself up to these parts again (or maybe for the first time) and feel your shame with-out judging it. You'll work toward releasing shame that has been keeping you stuck in withdrawal and disconnection, so you can build a layer of self-compassion for your healing journey.

Facing your shame will likely feel uncomfortable. Remember to take it slowly, allowing yourself to gradually access more of your shame, build your tolerance to it, and ultimately release it.

"Healing involves recognizing that your feelings of shame or unworthiness are directly connected to your undeniably legitimate human needs for connection."

—ARIELLE SCHWARTZ

Tanya's Story: Finding Freedom from Shame

Tanya sought therapy to work through relationship struggles, persistent thoughts of self-harm, and feelings of social anxiety and depression. She shared some of her history with her therapist, including that her parents were emotionally distant as well as reactive. After working with her therapist for a month or so, Tanya, with a bowed head and avoiding eye contact, shared that she had experienced years of emotional and sexual abuse as a child. Tanya's therapist thanked her for sharing this, and they gently began processing this together to help Tanya heal from it.

This was the first time Tanya had told anyone about her abuse. She had kept it inside for so long, and feared that anyone she told would judge her. But she felt supported and cared for when she told her therapist. That alone was such a relief for Tanya, and this was the first step that allowed her to slowly release the shame she felt about her past and start to believe that what happened was not her fault.

She continued to work with her therapist and also joined a support group with other trauma survivors, which helped her feel less and less alone. Feeling less shame and less alone decreased her self-critical thoughts and ideas of self-harm, improved her mood, and allowed her to gently let her walls down and become more open and vulnerable. This improved Tanya's relationships with others and with herself. She continues to work through her past abuse and the resulting trauma responses, but Tanya's overall well-being has significantly improved.

SOOTHING SHAME

Research shows that self-compassion is a powerful antidote to shame. For a trauma survivor who's lived with deep shame and closed off access to their vulnerability, it can be especially difficult to receive compassion from yourself or others. If you feel resistance to the self-compassion practices throughout this book, you're not alone. I encourage you to consider keeping an open mind about how self-compassion can be a healing tool for you.

Self-soothing practices are important tools as you begin to show yourself compassion and work through shame and trauma. This exercise will provide you with a variety of healthy self-soothing practices you can use to safely regulate your emotions and soothe shame.

Make a check mark next to the self-soothing practices you already use, then circle any others you would like to start using, or write your own in the space provided.

☐ Listen to soothing sounds or music

☐ Give yourself a hug while gently rocking or swaying

☐ Use a calming smell (for example, a scented candle or aromatherapy oil)

☐ Cuddle a stuffed animal, pillow, or pet

☐ Use a weighted blanket

☐ Think about your favorite things (movie, color, season, or something else)

☐ Do a deep-breathing exercise (see page 35)

☐ Take a warm bath or shower

☐ Do gentle physical movement (for example, walk or stretch)

☐ Use a self-soothing word or phrase (such as *Breathe* or *I can handle this*)

☐ Other: _____

☐ Other: _____

☐ Other: _____

EXPLORING YOUR FEELINGS OF SHAME

Toxic shame results from taking on and internalizing critical or devaluing messages from our culture, family, or others through direct or indirect experiences.

These messages can become internalized unconsciously when your sense of self is vulnerable, such as when you are a child and are still developing your identity, or when you receive repeated critical messages that break down your sense of self. For example, if you have a parent who frequently made negative comments about your intelligence, you may internalize a sense of shame about your abilities without even realizing where it came from. Women may receive these kinds of messages about circumstances such as being single, not having children, or speaking up for themselves.

1. **What critical or devaluing messages have you heard that have now become a part of you?**

   _____

   _____

   _____

2. **How have these messages affected your view of yourself, others, and the world?**

   _____

   _____

   _____

3. **How could your well-being and/or relationships improve if you were able to release your shame?**

   _____

   _____

   _____

IDENTIFYING SHAME IN YOUR BODY

Shame can be stored in your body even before you are able to speak, such as if your caregiver turned away from you when you needed their comfort as an infant. It's important to get in touch with how and where shame is stored in your body so you can better understand, regulate, and soothe it, even when your mind doesn't remember its roots.

Bring a situation or a thought to mind that brings with it mild to moderate shame (such as *I'm not enough*). Sit with this feeling for an amount of time that feels tolerable—maybe one minute—and notice where you feel the shame in your body.

Now mark on the image provided where you feel this shame.

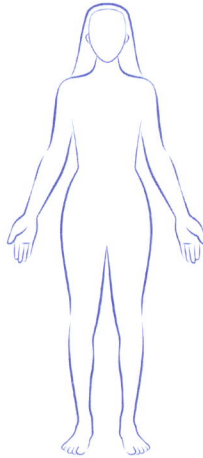

In addition to what you feel inside, shame in your body can be observed from the outside. Check the boxes that most closely describe your experience.

☐ Slumping your shoulders   ☐ Heart racing

☐ Nervously smiling   ☐ Sweating

☐ Hiding your eyes   ☐ Blushing

BREATHE IN COMPASSION, BREATHE OUT SHAME

Bringing your awareness to shame enables you to know you're feeling shame while you're feeling it. When your shame is no longer hidden, you can make space for it and begin to heal. You can begin to do this safely not by jumping into the deep end of your shame but by gently dipping your toes in with this mindfulness exercise:

1. Close your eyes or soften your gaze and take three slow, deep breaths.
2. Bring to mind a situation in which you experience mild to moderate feelings of shame.
3. Allow yourself to be present with this shame. Take a moment to notice any physical sensations you experience in your body.
4. Allow yourself to be fully present with your shame, without judgment, and to become an observer of this feeling.
5. Allow yourself to sit with your feelings and breathe through them for one to two minutes (if you can).
6. Now, with each slow, deep inhale, imagine yourself breathing in compassion for yourself. With each slow, deep exhale, imagine yourself breathing out shame.
7. Continue until you feel ready to open your eyes and bring your focus back to your surroundings.

BEHIND THE VOICE OF SHAME

You may have started to recognize self-critical thoughts that are lying beneath your shame (such as *I'm useless* or *I always make mistakes*). Some of these thoughts may have formed from the inaccurate narratives you've told yourself as a result of traumatic experiences you've had; others may be based on what has been said to you. It's not uncommon to carry the voice and words of people who have criticized or shamed you. It's important to remember these are thoughts driven by feelings of shame, traumatic experiences you've had, and critical messages you've received, not facts.

1. Write down three of the most common self-critical thoughts you have.

   _____

   _____

   _____

2. Whose voice are these thoughts speaking from (your own, a caregiver, a romantic partner)?

   _____

   _____

   _____

   _____

3. Who would you be if you could let these critical thoughts go?

   _____

   _____

   _____

   _____

ONE SMALL STEP AT A TIME

At the heart of shame is a deep desire for love, connection, and acceptance. Self-compassion can help open you up to receive these from yourself and others.

It takes time to move from shame and self-criticism to self-compassion. There will be many small steps along the way. This can be difficult for trauma survivors to accept, because trauma can result in all-or-nothing thinking: Either you feel worthwhile or you don't. Either you're self-compassionate or you're not.

Finding some middle ground in your thoughts and feelings can help you offer yourself more compassion. Use this exercise as a helpful next step to continue letting go of shame:

Draw an X on each line in the place that most closely represents how you feel today. Try not to judge where you place your X, because no matter where it is today, it may be in a different place tomorrow.

Come back to this exercise each day this week (and again whenever you'd like after that) to see how where you place your X changes. Notice what helps move your X toward the right and what moves it to the left.

How worthwhile do I feel today?

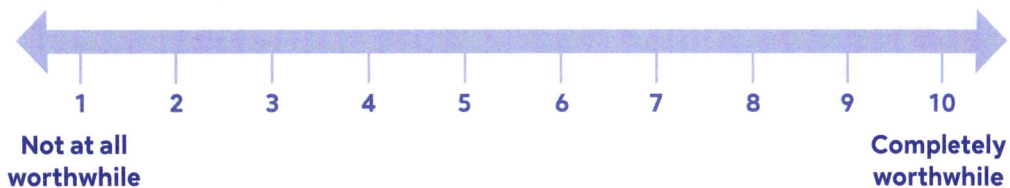

1   2   3   4   5   6   7   8   9   10

Not at all worthwhile   **Completely worthwhile**

How self-compassionate do I feel today?

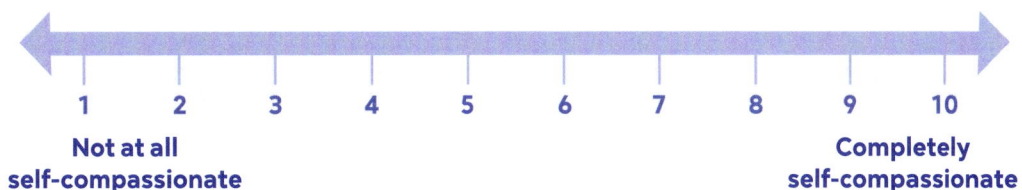

1   2   3   4   5   6   7   8   9   10

Not at all self-compassionate   **Completely self-compassionate**

COMFORTING YOUR INNER CHILD

Shame makes it very difficult for you to see yourself clearly. Instead, you view yourself through the distorted lens that was shaped by society, others, experiences, and eventually even yourself, which has said you are flawed or unworthy in some way.

Experiences such as separation, isolation, disconnection, and abuse can trigger shame. Think about a younger version of yourself who had an experience that triggered feelings of mild to moderate shame. What do you want to say to your younger self about the shame she's feeling? What did you need to hear when you were feeling that shame?

_____

_____

_____

_____

_____

_____

_____

How does it feel to accept those words?

_____

_____

_____

_____

_____

_____

_____

VULNERABILITY IS A SUPERPOWER

Shame keeps you small and quiet out of fear of being judged, criticized, or devalued by others. This may lead you to shut off access to your vulnerability and authenticity. Doing this protects you in unsafe situations.

Unfortunately, some people will judge you for anything and everything. You may have even encountered some of them in your life. Remaining closed off from them will keep you safe from their judgment. But shutting off all vulnerability can prevent you from finding people who will accept you for exactly who you are, and it feeds into the cycle of shame in which you feel flawed or unlovable.

Let's practice strengthening your vulnerability by opening up with a safe person.

1. Choose a safe person whom you believe will listen to you without judgment.
2. Choose one topic to share with them that brings you mild feelings of shame.
3. Choose a safe environment (physical or virtual) in which to talk with your safe person.

Tips for practicing vulnerability:

- **Start with a topic that may feel uncomfortable, but which is tolerable, to share.**

- **Focus on making a connection with the person you're speaking with rather than making an impression or winning their approval.**

TURN UP THE VOLUME ON SELF-COMPASSION

Are you often critical of yourself? This may be a legacy of the past, when blaming yourself gave you a sense of control in situations that felt totally out of your control. Sometimes, even years later, the volume is turned up so loud on your critical inner voice that you cannot hear your self-compassionate voice. Thankfully, through practice and patience, you can strengthen and turn up the volume of your kinder inner voice.

Bring to mind a recent situation in which your critical inner voice has shown up. Then, in the left-hand column of the following table, write down three things your inner critic has to say about what happened. In the right-hand column, write different, self-compassionate responses to each statement.

Challenge yourself to use each of the three components of self-compassion in your responses: mindfulness (awareness without judgment), common humanity (remembering everyone struggles and you're not alone), and kindness.

SELF-CRITICAL VOICE	SELF-COMPASSIONATE VOICE
Example: I can't believe I forgot to do that. I'm so stupid.	*Example: I'm feeling shame but I'm not stupid; everyone makes mistakes.*

PERFECTLY IMPERFECT

Attempting to be "perfect" can emerge from inner shame as a way to cope with perceived flaws and to protect you from rejection, criticism, or hurt. Perfectionism tends to outlive its initial purpose, however, and it can become a barrier to living freely and fully without the fear of failure.

1. List five small ways you can be imperfect (for example, take the wrong exit off the freeway, wear mismatched socks) and commit to doing them this week.

    _____

    _____

    _____

    _____

    _____

2. When you have done all five, reflect on how it felt to allow yourself to be imperfect.

    _____

    _____

    _____

    _____

3. How do you think life could be easier if you allowed yourself the grace to be imperfect in the future?

    _____

    _____

    _____

    _____

REVEALING THE LAYERS OF YOU

We all have different parts of ourselves we share with or hide from others to varying degrees. When you're carrying shame, you may be likely to hide more parts than you share. In this exercise, you'll explore different parts of yourself and how you share or hide them from different people in your life. This can help you see what parts of yourself you've hidden (and to what extent) and deepen your understanding of what parts you might be experiencing as shameful.

On each layer of the cake, provide a brief description of each version of you. For example, the you that everyone sees may be very agreeable, while the you that only you see is much more opinionated. Or the you people see when they first meet you might be very serious, while the you that only the person closest to you sees is silly and has a good sense of humor.

1. **Frosting:** The you that everyone sees
2. **First layer:** The you that people see when they first meet you
3. **Second layer:** The you that only your closest person sees (a friend, family member, or partner)
4. **Third layer:** The you that only you see
5. **Fourth layer:** The you that's still hidden: things about yourself that you don't know yet or parts that are still too tender to reveal themselves and may carry the most amount of shame (you may not be aware of these hidden parts yet; feel free to add them later)

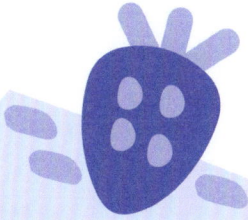

Who Everyone Sees

First Impressions of You

Who Your Closest Person Sees

Who Only You See

Who's Still Hidden

EMBRACE SELF-ACCEPTANCE

Self-acceptance means fully embracing yourself exactly as you are, without judgment. When you accept yourself, not only do you build confidence and worthiness within yourself, you are also able to connect with others with more authenticity and presence.

Try this creative exercise to help release shame and embrace your true self. Fill the inside of the circle with images, words, and colors that represent your shame, including limiting beliefs, self-criticisms, and anything else you can think of. Surround the outside of the circle with images, words, and colors that represent what you'd like to begin accepting about yourself, including traits, personal values, and any other skills and strengths you possess.

A LETTER TO RELEASE YOUR SHAME

Shame will not go away completely, and it doesn't need to. Feeling the full spectrum of emotions is what allows us to heal. But you can change your relationship to shame by using compassion and other healthy skills, so that it releases its grip on you and your life.

To continue releasing shame, write a letter to the part of yourself that is carrying shame, or write a letter to someone who you've felt shamed by. If it feels tolerable, you might read this letter aloud to yourself, to a safe person, or to an empty chair representing the person you felt shamed by.

_____

_____

_____

_____

_____

_____

_____

_____

_____

_____

_____

_____

_____

_____

_____

_____

My past may hurt a lot, but it does not define me. I am deserving of love, connection, and acceptance.

KEY TAKEAWAYS

Whatever trauma happened to you was not your fault. Feeling shame as a result of what happened to you is not your fault, either. Allowing nonjudgmental space for your shame through mindfulness, compassion, and getting in touch with where shame is in your body will help you improve your relationship to shame and safely release it.

- We use shame to attempt to provide meaning and a sense of control in situations where we otherwise feel powerless, overwhelmed, and confused.

- At the heart of shame is a deep desire for love, connection, and acceptance, and self-compassion can help open us up to receive these from ourselves and others.

- Through practice and patience, we can strengthen and turn up the volume of our compassionate inner voice.

- Gaining self-acceptance enables us to build confidence and worthiness within ourselves and to connect to others with more authenticity and presence.

SECTION 4
EXPLORING EMOTIONS

Emotions are powerful. They show us what truly matters, guide us in making choices, help us connect with others, and make life more meaningful. But as someone who has lived through trauma, you may find your emotions sometimes feel out of balance.

Dr. Gabor Maté, a physician who studies addiction, trauma, and stress, describes trauma as leaving people with both an open wound and a scar. The open wound can make you extra sensitive to perceived danger, causing you to feel like the traumatic event is happening all over again. The scar creates a thick layer that numbs and disconnects you from your emotions, your body, others, and the world around you. This provides a beautiful, and possibly painfully relatable, explanation of the impact of trauma on your emotions.

In this section of the book, we'll explore both sides of this legacy, helping you safely get in touch with your feelings and learn skills to bring your emotions into balance. You'll also gain a stronger understanding of the triggers that bring up intense emotions, how to cope with them, and how to observe your feelings mindfully. Let's remember to ride the waves of your emotions safely and at a pace that works for you. One step at a time, you'll learn to better connect to your emotions without getting stuck in or overwhelmed by them as you continue your healing journey.

> "Inviting our thoughts and feelings into awareness allows us to learn from them rather than be driven by them."
> —DANIEL J. SIEGEL

Je'nay's Story: Feeling Her Feelings Again

Je'nay was a highly sensitive, emotional, sweet child. Unfortunately, while she was growing up, her parents constantly invalidated or dismissed her emotions. She wasn't allowed to cry, and she was misunderstood or neglected when she would express any "negative" emotions. She was often told to "toughen up" and labeled as "too sensitive." Je'nay's parents didn't teach her how to manage her emotions, probably because they didn't know how to manage their own. Instead, they taught her how to deny and bury them, and that her emotions were "too much" for anyone to handle, including herself.

As a result, Je'nay developed unhealthy coping skills at an early age and had difficulty feeling and validating her own emotions. She struggled to feel her emotions without becoming consumed by them, so she chose to avoid or minimize them by saying that what she was feeling "wasn't that bad" and using avoidance coping skills such as mindlessly scrolling on her phone. Je'nay also found herself repeating unhealthy relationship patterns as she searched for the validation she didn't receive from her parents or from herself. She often stayed with partners who took advantage of her emotionally and financially but gave her the attention she desperately longed for.

Within the safe relationship she developed with her therapist, Je'nay has been able to begin to really feel her emotions again and learn the skills to bring her intense feelings into balance. She has also started to understand that she was never "too much," but rather that her parents did not have the skills or capacity to care for her emotional needs. She is now on her way to finding more self-acceptance, fulfillment, and joy.

NAME IT TO TAME IT

Emotional regulation is the ability to respond to and manage your feelings in a healthy, balanced way. Trauma can make it hard to regulate emotions by disconnecting you from them; instead, you prioritize survival and protect yourself from real or perceived threats, including big emotions. Trauma can also disrupt the emotion center of your brain, the amygdala, which can become overactive and leave you feeling your feelings so strongly that they overwhelm you.

The six main emotional states are widely believed to be happiness, surprise, anger, fear, sadness, and disgust. Many secondary emotions, such as anxiety stemming from fear, relate to each of these primary emotions.. In this exercise, you will label your emotions and attach colors to them to help get in touch with what you are feeling, observe from a distance what comes up, and help your amygdala become less reactive to strong emotions.

For each set of emotions, choose a color that resonates most with you. (For example, if you choose red for Anger, you'll fill in Anger, Frustrated, Annoyed, Critical, and Resentful in red.) Over the next week, use this wheel to practice labeling your emotions each day. At the end of each day, circle the main emotions you felt during that day. After this week, come back to your emotion wheel as often as you need to.

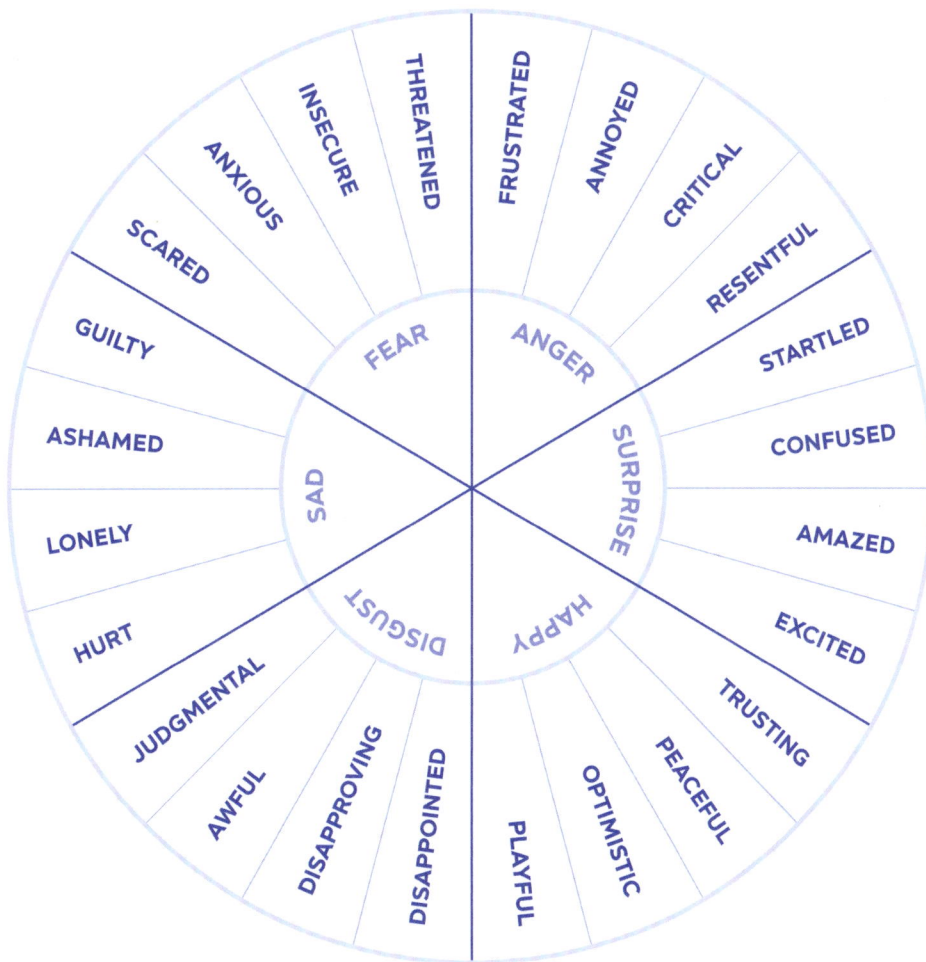

The emotion wheel. Inner ring: FEAR, ANGER, SURPRISE, HAPPY, DISGUST, SAD.

FEAR: THREATENED, INSECURE, ANXIOUS, SCARED
ANGER: FRUSTRATED, ANNOYED, CRITICAL, RESENTFUL
SURPRISE: STARTLED, CONFUSED, AMAZED
HAPPY: EXCITED, TRUSTING, PEACEFUL, OPTIMISTIC, PLAYFUL
DISGUST: DISAPPOINTED, DISAPPROVING, AWFUL, JUDGMENTAL
SAD: HURT, LONELY, ASHAMED, GUILTY

HEY EMOTIONS, I'D LIKE TO GET TO KNOW YOU

Do you sometimes find it hard to be aware of your emotions? You may find your trauma has left you disconnected from your feelings, perhaps for quite some time. This can be especially true for women, who more often experience the types of trauma that more significantly affect emotional regulation. For example, we are more likely to live through early trauma in childhood, as well as intimate partner violence as adults.

You may not know what each emotion looks and feels like for you. If this is true, there's no judgment here. Your difficulty accepting and feeling your emotions developed as a survival strategy. Now that you're here to heal, try giving yourself permission to start letting go of the strategies you needed to keep you safe, so that you can really start to live.

Use the following table to begin reconnecting with your emotions by raising your awareness and understanding of them. Imagine a situation in which each emotion comes up for you at a tolerable level (for example, you might feel happiness when you do your favorite activity). Then reflect on and notice what thoughts, body sensations, and behaviors come up for you when you feel that emotion. Fill out the table with as much detail as you are aware of now. You can add to it as you learn more and become more connected to your emotions.

	WHAT THOUGHTS DO YOU HAVE?	WHAT BODILY SENSATIONS DO YOU HAVE?	WHAT BEHAVIORS DO YOU HAVE?
Happiness			
Surprise			
Anger			
Fear			
Sadness			
Disgust			

A SAFE CONTAINER

Containment can help you safely manage emotional distress by storing away troubling thoughts, emotions, sensations, and memories to revisit later. Rather than suppressing your emotions, which involves ignoring or avoiding them without any intention of addressing them, containment is meant to hold these troubling thoughts, emotions, sensations, and memories until you're ready to process them fully. This may be helpful when they come up at a time or place where you cannot address them, such as during work or at a family event, or when you're feeling over-whelmed and recognize that it will be safer for you to process your emotions when you're more relaxed. Containment can also be useful when you have something you'd like to process with your therapist or another safe person; your container can hold it for you until you talk to them.

I invite you to practice containment by spending some time writing about something distressing that's on your mind that you would like to come back to at a later time. When you're finished, close your journal to represent closing the lid of your container. It can be helpful to have an image of a container in your mind (any container that can be closed, such as a safe or a jewelry box) and imagine safely closing your distress-ing emotions into it.

_____

_____

_____

_____

_____

_____

_____

_____

HEALING THE PAST TO CONNECT WITH THE PRESENT

Have you ever had an emotional reaction that didn't seem to make sense? For example, your partner calmly asked if you took out the garbage and you blew up at them. This kind of mismatched reaction can be due to something triggering an old emotion that hasn't been processed.

Healing the significant emotions from your past will help you have a healthy, connected relationship with your current emotions. To explore this, let's start by focusing on increasing your awareness and understanding of your triggers, so you can begin to notice past emotions that still need to heal.

1. **Bring to mind one time you experienced a trigger in the past few weeks (or any other time). Trauma triggers can be a person, place, sound, smell, taste, situation, time of year, emotion, memory, sensation, word, or image associated with a past traumatic event. Focus on a trigger that feels tolerable to think and write about below.**

_____

_____

_____

2. **Get curious about this trigger and answer the following:**
    How did my body respond to the trigger (heart pounding, chest feeling tight, something else)? What thoughts and emotions came with the trigger? When have I experienced something like this before?

_____

_____

_____

YOUR EARLY EXPERIENCES

The ways you manage your emotions are often strongly influenced by your early experiences, including those that are challenging, such as being repeatedly ridiculed when expressing your emotions or growing up in an environment where your caregivers or other influential people avoided expressing their emotions or used unhealthy coping skills (such as drinking too much alcohol or lashing out at others) to manage their feelings.

1. Reflecting on your early experiences can help you better understand your current ability to regulate emotions. How did the people around you seem to express, feel, and cope with their emotions?

_____

_____

_____

_____

_____

_____

2. How were your emotions handled in childhood (for example, were they met with compassion, judgment, invalidation)?

_____

_____

_____

_____

_____

_____

SETTING FAIR EXPECTATIONS

Sometimes we have unrealistic expectations about our emotions, such as believing we should always feel happy, that experiencing emotions in extremes is the only way to feel them, or that we're only supposed to feel one emotion at a time. This doesn't leave room to feel all our emotions as they are, and it can contribute to feelings of shame when our experience doesn't fit our expectations.

1. What expectations do you have for your emotions?

_____

_____

_____

_____

2. In what ways might these expectations be affecting you negatively?

_____

_____

_____

_____

3. How can you adjust your expectations so they have a positive effect on you and how you regulate your emotions?

_____

_____

_____

_____

DRAW YOUR SAFE SPACE

Have you ever been gripped by a sudden, strong emotion, such as fear, shame, or anger, that didn't seem to match up with the situation you were in? It's possible you were experiencing an emotional flashback. These are brought on by triggers from your past, and often include emotions such as intense bouts of fear, shame, despair, sadness, or anger. For example, you might feel a sudden wave of intense shame when you make a minor mistake at work due to the constant harsh criticism you used to receive from your ex-partner.

Grounding techniques are amazing tools to help you cope with both triggers and emotional flashbacks. They use your senses to help bring you back to the present moment, reminding you that you are safe now. These tools can be used just about anywhere, anytime.

One tool is to draw your safe space. Take a minute to imagine a safe space where you can go to feel grounded and secure whenever you need. When you can see it clearly in your mind, draw it in the space provided on the following page with as much detail as possible. Include images and words that describe how your safe space looks, smells, sounds, and feels. (If the term *safe space* doesn't work for you, you can call it your calm, peaceful, or comforting space instead.)

The next time you experience a trigger or an emotional flashback, or have another distressing experience, bring your safe space to mind to shift you into the present. This safe space is available to you now anytime you need it.

LEARN TO DANCE IN THE RAIN

Sometimes we can confuse passing emotions for permanent facts. Our minds like to create stories from feelings because that gives us a false sense of control. For example, you may feel that you are going to be unsuccessful when you do a presentation at work, and then incorrectly believe this is an unavoidable fact. It's not the result you want, but at least you have removed the uncertainty.

One way to avoid turning feelings into false stories is to observe your emotions with compassion, and to allow them to come and go without trying to resist them. The RAIN exercise, created by psychologist Tara Brach, can help you practice this. Find a comfortable position, bring to mind a mildly challenging experience, and follow these steps:

1. **Recognize:** Bring presence and awareness to this moment, including current thoughts, emotions, and sensations.
2. **Allow:** Let the thoughts, emotions, and sensations be there just as they are, without judgment.
3. **Investigate:** Get curious about this moment by asking yourself: *Is there something that needs my attention? Where do I feel this sensation in my body? What does this vulnerable place want from me?*

4. **Nurture:** Try to get a sense of what this place inside you needs and offer it some care and compassion. Treat yourself as you would a friend in distress, with kind words and actions.

GET FRIENDLY WITH YOUR NERVOUS SYSTEM

Your nervous system plays a vital role in how your body and mind function, and it also plays an important role in trauma recovery. In this exercise, we'll explore the role your nervous system plays in regulating emotions and how it responds to trauma.

You know that feeling when stressors pile up and you get overwhelmed and lose control? Maybe you're running late for work and you drop your keys in between the car seats and let out a scream, or you have a difficult phone call with your parent and then see that your partner forgot to put a new bag in the empty garbage can and yell at them. This is what it feels like to pass your **window of tolerance**.

When you are inside your window of tolerance, your nervous system can handle stress in a healthy way. You feel safe, stable, and secure and are able to regulate your emotions without becoming overwhelmed.

When you go past your window of tolerance, you go into either **hyperarousal** (in which your fight-or-flight response is activated) or **hypoarousal** (in which your shutdown response is activated). In hyperarousal, you may become overwhelmed with anger or anxiety, feel on edge or irritable, and have difficulty sleeping. In hypoarousal, you may isolate, feel numb, and lack interest in activities you usually enjoy.

With trauma, your window of tolerance can shrink, which means you may go into hyperarousal or hypoarousal more quickly and frequently. The good news is that you can expand your window of tolerance by using practices such as mindfulness, deep breathing, grounding techniques, physical movement, and other healthy coping skills.

Understanding how you experience each nervous system state (window of tolerance, hyperarousal, and hypoarousal) will help you recognize when you're experiencing them and be better able to find regulation and balance. To help you do this, read through the traits listed on page 62 for each nervous system state and circle which you recognize in yourself when you experience each state.

continued on next page

continued from previous page

Window of Tolerance (Safe and Connected)

- Grounded in the present moment
- Calm, safe, and secure
- Able to manage stressors effectively
- Able to regulate emotions and self-soothe
- Able to be engaged and connect with others
- You're in your comfort zone
- Making eye contact with others
- Normal breathing

Hyperarousal (Fight or Flight)

- Increased energy
- Overwhelmed with anger or rage
- On edge with fear, panic, or anxiety
- Busy mind with racing thoughts
- Difficulty concentrating
- Find it harder to engage and connect with others
- Faster breathing
- Restlessness and/or difficulty sleeping

Hypoarousal (Shutdown)

- Decreased energy
- Depressed mood
- Numbness of emotions
- Loss of interest in activities
- Helplessness or hopelessness
- Disconnected from self and others
- Slowed breathing
- Diminished eye contact with others

EXPAND YOUR WINDOW OF TOLERANCE

Here are some strategies you can use to expand your window of tolerance. For the next week, choose one or a few you would like to use each day. Write your choices on the lines below. At the end of the week, write down which strategies you found helpful and which new ones you'd like to try next.

☐ Hum or sing

☐ Notice signs of safety around you

☐ Vent by journaling about all your feelings

☐ Tapping (see page 98)

☐ Notice how you feel, without judgment

☐ Sleep for seven to nine hours

☐ Take a fifteen- to twenty-minute walk

☐ Do a breathing exercise

☐ Practice a self-soothing exercise

☐ Say five kind things about yourself

☐ Express three things you're grateful for

☐ Connect with a safe loved one

_____

_____

_____

_____

_____

_____

_____

_____

_____

_____

_____

YOUR GLIMMER JOURNAL

Glimmers are small, everyday moments that help bring a sense of calm, relaxation, and safety to your nervous system, such as feeling the warmth of the sun. They are the opposite of triggers. While they can easily go unnoticed, once you learn to spot them, you'll see that they're all around you, and you can begin looking for more.

Use this space to keep a glimmer journal for the next week. Intentionally look for glimmers, and make note of each one you experience and where, who you're with, and how you feel when you experience it, so you can begin to notice patterns that will help you continue to see more.

Day 1: _____

_____

Day 2: _____

_____

Day 3: _____

_____

Day 4: _____

_____

Day 5: _____

_____

Day 6: _____

_____

Day 7: _____

_____

IT'S OKAY TO BE EMOTIONAL

Like so many women, you probably have been told to "calm down" or "stop being so emotional" when you've expressed strong feelings. We live in a culture that prizes being stoic and minimizing big emotions. Because of this, your anger may be seen as irrational, your distress as an overreaction, your crying as a weakness, and so on.

1. **How have you experienced this attitude at home, at work, and in the world?**

_____

_____

_____

_____

_____

_____

2. **How can you challenge these societal expectations through a lens of compassion and acceptance for your emotions? What thoughts or actions might help you challenge them, so you can begin to see your emotions as strengths rather than weaknesses?**

_____

_____

_____

_____

_____

_____

_____

TUNE IN TO YOUR NERVOUS SYSTEM

Sometimes you feel calmer, relaxed, and connected. Sometimes you feel more angry, anxious, or on edge, and other times you feel more shut down and disconnected. All these states have their purpose. For example, anger might be telling you that an injustice is being done or a boundary is being crossed (or needs to be set). Shutdown might be letting you know that you're under significant stress or facing danger and need to step away. Music can affect all these states by regulating your nervous system and releasing feel-good chemicals in your brain, resulting in decreased stress and better relaxation, mood regulation, and social connection.

Create two playlists. When you feel safe, relaxed, grounded, and connected to yourself and others, choose songs that promote feelings of calm, excitement, connection, celebration, and joy to deepen your connection to this state. Write these songs under your Window-of-Tolerance Playlist.

When you feel angry, anxious, on edge, and irritable or shut down, hopeless, low on energy, or disconnected from yourself and others, choose songs that represent anxiety, anger, low energy, disconnection, and survival. Tuning in to them will help teach your body there are safe ways to connect with all your emotions and sensations, including those you might be inclined to avoid or be scared to feel. Write these songs under your Fight-or-Flight/Shutdown Playlist.

I've started both lists with a song that works for me. Add as many songs as you'd like to each of your playlists.

WINDOW-OF-TOLERANCE PLAYLIST

"I Wanna Dance with Somebody (Who Loves Me)" by Whitney Houston

_____

_____

_____

_____

_____

_____

_____

FIGHT-OR-FLIGHT/SHUTDOWN PLAYLIST

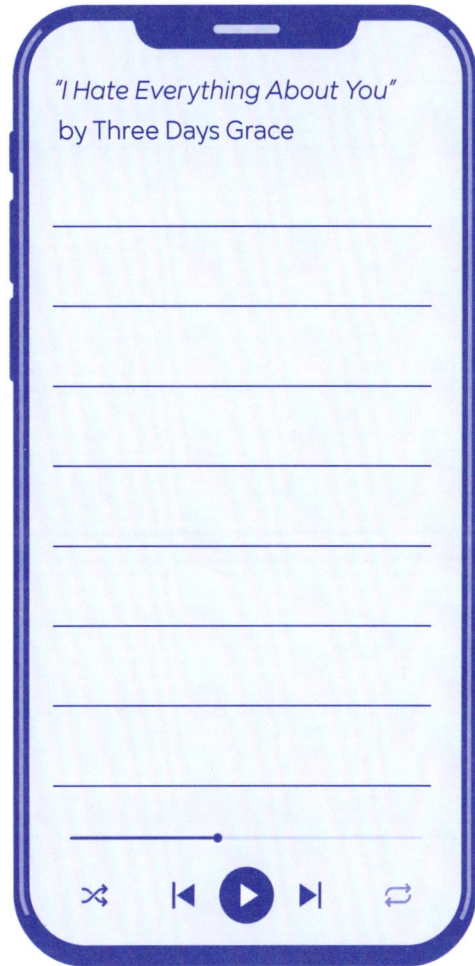

"I Hate Everything About You" by Three Days Grace

_____

_____

_____

_____

_____

_____

_____

YOU'RE WORTHY OF FEELING GREAT

It's not just uncomfortable emotions that are hard to feel and accept. Even comfortable ones, such as happiness and joy, are sometimes difficult to let in. This may be because you don't feel worthy of feeling good or your experiences have taught you that all emotions are big and scary and not safe to feel. This mindful imagery practice can help you begin to feel and accept, and actually enhance, the experience of your comfortable emotions.

1. Find a comfortable position, close your eyes or soften your gaze, and take three slow, deep breaths in and out.
2. As vividly as possible, bring to mind the feeling of any comfortable emotions you experienced today (or this week).
3. Begin to slowly intensify these emotions. Gradually allow yourself to feel them more deeply, by imagining them growing bigger within you or connecting with where you feel them in your body.
4. Remain with the sense of these comfortable emotions and experience the bodily sensations that accompany them.
5. Try not to change or avoid the emotions and sensations; just notice and experience them. Tell each of them, "You belong here."
6. Now, sense that these comfortable emotions are beginning to sink deeply into you, growing and becoming a part of you.
7. Breathe into those places where the emotions are, and continue to sense them sinking into you.
8. When you feel ready, open your eyes and bring your focus back to your surroundings.

CONNECTING WITH GRIEF

Grief is the emotional response to the loss of someone or something important. A vast amount of grief can come with trauma, and it's important to acknowledge and care for it, just as you are learning to do with your other emotions. Loss and grief are different for every person and every traumatic experience, but some trauma-related losses you might be grieving include loss of childhood, loss of safety, loss of self, and loss of relationships.

1. **What have you lost as a result of the trauma you've experienced?**

   _____

   _____

   _____

   _____

2. **Where do you feel the grief in your body?**

   _____

   _____

   _____

   _____

3. **What will help you process this grief?**

   _____

   _____

   _____

   _____

I create space to heal my emotions. My emotions matter and they do not control me.

KEY TAKEAWAYS

Trauma can affect how you feel, express, connect, manage, and respond to your emotions in many ways. As a result, you've likely developed protective survival strategies that have made it harder to balance your emotions. Give yourself permission to start gently letting go of those strategies and to continue practicing healthy emotional skills so you can safely ride the waves of your feelings.

- Trauma can affect your ability to manage emotions by disconnecting you from your feelings or by causing you to experience them so strongly that they feel overwhelming.

- Healing the painful emotions from your past will help you have a healthy, connected relationship with your current emotions.

- Safety, healthy coping skills, and healing can expand your window of tolerance, increasing your ability to manage and respond to stress.

- Regulating your nervous system has many benefits, including improved emotional regulation.

- As you continue healing, you can learn to accept all your emotions, not just the really uncomfortable emotions but also the comfortable ones.

EMBRACING SELF-CARE

Embracing self-care is an important part of your healing journey, but it's also difficult for many trauma survivors. Maybe you've been in situations where your needs were treated as an inconvenience, and you learned to stop asking for or even paying attention to what you need. Or maybe you had to be so focused on survival there wasn't space or time to develop healthy coping or self-care practices, so now your needs seem completely unfamiliar to you. Your experiences also may have affected your self-worth, which can lead to feeling you're not worth taking care of.

Additionally, because women are often raised to be caregivers, we're put in positions where we're responsible for others and expected to prioritize others' needs, sometimes starting at a very young age. It's no wonder so many women struggle with practicing self-care and putting themselves first.

This section will help demystify self-care and offer everyday ways to practice it. You'll uncover how to prioritize self-care by exploring your needs, learning about healthy and unhealthy coping skills, and caring for your inner child. You'll come away with tools that you can start using now to help you throughout your journey.

"Take care of yourself as if you're the most awesome person you've ever met."

—JEN SINCERO

Hyunju's Story: Discovering She's Worth Caring For

When Hyunju started therapy, she was having trouble establishing healthy habits and taking care of herself. She also struggled with identifying her purpose and having self-critical thoughts that led to thoughts about self-harm. While exploring all this with Hyunju, it became clear that there was a history of emotional neglect in her life. She described her parents as nice people who had their own struggles with mental health and emotional availability. Because they didn't express their own emotions, they couldn't teach Hyunju how to process hers. Because they didn't show love (at least not in ways that Hyunju could recognize), she didn't develop healthy self-worth and had a really hard time being vulnerable.

Hyunju was so closed off to others, and even to herself, that she often felt lonely, even when she was with friends and family. This further contributed to her low self-worth, and she didn't feel worthy of taking care of herself or making herself a priority. She struggled to create healthy habits, such as getting enough sleep and keeping her living space clean, and often questioned her purpose or motivation for waking up in the morning.

Slowly, Hyunju learned how to be vulnerable with herself and with others, starting by choosing one or two safe people to practice opening up to and gradually sharing more of herself with them. This greatly improved the depth of her current relationships and her ability to create new ones. It also built her confidence. As she began to feel more accepted by others, it opened the door for her to allow more self-worth and self-compassion and to work toward accepting herself. This has helped her decrease thoughts of self-harm and begin to slowly develop the healthy, daily self-care habits she wants.

SURVIVAL COPING SKILLS CHECKLIST

Coping with everyday life can be a challenge. But knowing how to cope with difficult experiences is even more challenging, especially if you don't have support during or soon after those experiences.

As a result of trauma, you may have developed certain skills to help you manage overwhelming emotions, memories, and mind-body responses. Some of these may be unhealthy coping skills. These tend to fall into the categories of avoidance, hypervigilance, and risky behaviors. Although unhealthy, these strategies helped you survive. But because they offer only short-term relief rather than true healing, continuing to use them keeps you in a cycle of dysregulation, low self-esteem, and, sometimes, dangerous circumstances.

Becoming more aware of which of these skills you may be using and showing yourself compassion and understanding for using them are important steps in your healing process. Check off as many of these common unhealthy trauma coping skills as you currently use.

☐ Isolation

☐ Self-harm

☐ Self-criticism

☐ Overworking

☐ Excessive sleep

☐ Impulsive spending

☐ Overscheduling yourself

☐ Substance misuse or addictions

☐ Overthinking or excessive worry

☐ Distorted or emotional eating habits

☐ Hoarding (food, clothing, other items or resources)

☐ Binge-watching TV or mindlessly scrolling on social media

MAKE ROOM FOR THE NEW

Creating safety within yourself, your body, and your environment can help reduce your need for unhealthy coping strategies and make room for healthier ones. To get started, let's explore the barriers that might be holding you back from using new coping skills. From the skills you identified in the Survival Coping Skills Checklist, which one feels the hardest to let go of?

_____

What purpose has this coping skill served for you?

_____

_____

_____

_____

What are the challenges stopping you from letting it go?

_____

_____

_____

_____

How can you begin to make room for a healthier coping skill?

_____

_____

_____

_____

DAILY STRESS RELIEF

We face stress every day; it's an unavoidable part of life. Healthy amounts of stress help us get up in the morning and get our daily tasks done, but overwhelming amounts are harmful to our health.

When you experience stress, your body perceives a threat and initiates the stress-response cycle—your fight-or-flight response is activated. Sometimes this cycle closes on its own when the stressful event ends. Other times, especially with chronic stress and repeated trauma, the cycle persists and you may find yourself stuck in fight-or-flight mode. If that happens, you need to do something intentional to close the stress-response cycle.

In the table here, I've mixed up the stress-relief strategies and benefits. Can you figure out which benefit goes with each strategy? Draw a line from each strategy on the left side to the matching stress-relief benefits on the right side.

When you are done, check the answer key at the bottom of the page for the matching pairs. Then, choose one (or more) to use every day to help close your stress-response cycle.

WAYS TO RELIEVE STRESS	STRESS-RELIEF BENEFITS
Crying	Helps regulate emotions and ground you in the present moment
Laughing	Imitates the effects of stress and helps your body work through those effects
Creative Expression	Releases feel-good hormones, which can increase your ability to deal with stress
Positive Social Interaction	Increases endorphins and results in emotional and physical relaxation
Deep Breathing	A natural release that can help balance your nervous system
Physical Activity	Decreases heart rate and blood pressure and brings a feeling of calm

Answer key: 1e, 2d, 3a, 4c, 5f, 6b

SELF-CARE IS MORE THAN BUBBLE BATHS

Self-care is sometimes portrayed as bubble baths and mani-pedis. Sure, those can be helpful, but it's much more than that. True self-care includes the ways you care for your whole self: mentally, physically, emotionally, socially, and spiritually.

Although self-care may not have been acknowledged, prioritized, or viewed positively in your life up to now, true self-care is necessary for you to maintain your well-being. When you consistently put others first or otherwise ignore your needs, healing can be more difficult, and you can get stuck in self-neglect, which can harm your emotional well-being. The good news is you can start taking better care of yourself at any time.

Here is a list of self-care activities that are often overlooked and under-appreciated. Try to start small by adding one to your daily routine for the next week, then slowly build from there.

1. Stretch my body for ten minutes.
2. Drink enough water daily.
3. Floss my teeth daily.
4. Spend time in nature.
5. Get seven to nine hours of sleep each night.
6. Give myself extra time to get to places.
7. Take a moment to appreciate my surroundings.
8. Clean one small area in my living space.
9. Celebrate one small success each day.
10. Say no to things I don't want to do.
11. Enjoy calming scents with candles or aromatherapy.
12. Do something creative.
13. Make myself a healthy snack or meal.
14. Wake up earlier, for a slower start to my day.

ALLOW YOURSELF TO REST

Rest can feel like a threat to your system when you're in survival mode. But allowing yourself to rest is just as important for your healing journey as your other coping skills and self-care activities. This includes not only getting enough sleep, but also committing time to being alone, being in a quiet space, taking breaks from mentally and physically demanding tasks, and doing any other activities that help your mind and body relax and recover.

1. Reflect on a time when you gave yourself permission to rest and recharge mentally, physically, and/or emotionally. How did you feel before and after?

_____

_____

_____

_____

_____

_____

2. Moving forward, what are some ways you can you prioritize rest? What encouragement can you give yourself that it is necessary and safe to rest?

_____

_____

_____

_____

_____

_____

DECODING YOUR NEEDS

Have you ever skipped a meal or a bathroom break? I know I have. When you do that, you are ignoring your needs. Our most basic human needs are safety, love, and physiological needs; these include food, shelter, trust, affection, freedom from fear, and belonging to a group.

During traumatic experiences, these needs are often violated or not met, which can cloud your ability to identify them. Know that it's okay and normal to have needs, and remind yourself of this as often as necessary. Learning to understand your needs will help you incorporate self-care into your daily routine.

Create a Needs Cheat Sheet for yourself by starting with the six primary emotions. Reflect on times when you have felt each emotion listed in the first column. Then, in the second column, write down what you needed in that moment, or what you think you'll need, to care for yourself when you feel that emotion. For example, for Anger, you might write "Deep breathing, cry or other physical release, eat a snack." As you learn more about your needs, you can come back to this exercise to add to or change your responses

EMOTION	WHAT I NEED WHEN I'M FEELING THIS
Happiness	
Surprise	
Anger	
Fear	
Sadness	
Disgust	

YOUR NEEDS MATTER

Valuing and prioritizing your needs will help you be able to put yourself first more consistently. Choose one need you want to start valuing and prioritizing.

1. What has gotten in your way of valuing and prioritizing this need in the past?

    _____

    _____

    _____

    _____

    _____

2. How can you start valuing this need now?

    _____

    _____

    _____

    _____

    _____

3. Is it something you can do on your own, or do you require help from someone to get this need met? If help is needed, how can you communicate to get what you need from others?

    _____

    _____

    _____

    _____

    _____

VISUALIZING YOUR INNER CHILD

Every one of us has a young, vulnerable part of ourselves inside: an inner child. Your inner child may have had unmet needs and experiences that left wounds that remain unhealed and continue to affect your life today. Some possible signs of these wounds are difficulty being alone, difficulty asking for help, a strong need for external validation, and repressing emotions. Practice patience, compassion, and curiosity as you get familiar with your inner child's wounds and needs with this visualization:

1. Imagine yourself or view a picture of yourself at whatever age you first remember not feeling good enough.
2. Close your eyes or soften your gaze and take slow, deep breaths until you feel relaxed.
3. Imagine that younger version of yourself off in the distance.
4. Ask her if it's okay to sit with her. Let her know you're here to listen and understand her.
5. Ask what she needs from you in order to feel safe.
6. Allow yourself to listen to whatever responses come up.
7. Assure her you'll always be there for her whenever she needs you.
8. Imagine embracing her with a warm hug.
9. Know you can return to this visualization whenever you want to connect with her and thank her for connecting with you.
10. When you're ready, open your eyes and bring your focus back to your surroundings.

A CALENDAR OF CARE

Along with becoming familiar with your inner child's wounds, unmet needs, wants, and emotions, it's important to remember your inner child wants to be loved, cared for, and have some fun! Try these activities to reconnect with your inner child and tap into her freedom of expression, creativity, wonder, play, joy, and intuition.

SUN	Let loose with a solo dance party	Be a photographer for the day	Play a game you enjoyed as a child	Your choice!
MON	Paint using colors that represent your inner child	Blow bubbles	Try something new (such as a TV show or restaurant)	Sing your heart out
TUE	Spend time outside without distractions	Eat your favorite childhood snack or meal	Your choice!	Play with building blocks, modeling clay, or similar
WED	Your choice!	Laugh freely	Allow yourself to daydream	Make a playlist of your favorite music from childhood
THU	Watch a favorite movie from childhood	Take a mindful walk outside	Play a computer, video, or phone game	Wear an expressive outfit, accessory, or piece of clothing
FRI	Play a board or card game	Your choice!	Watch a favorite TV show from childhood	Draw a picture of your inner child
SAT	Learn something new (such as a recipe)	Write a creative short story about your inner child	Do something spontaneous	Engage in an outdoor activity you enjoy

A LETTER TO YOUR INNER CHILD

Getting to know your inner child is a transformational and challenging process. When it gets tough, I like to remind my clients, "Little you is so lucky to have you looking after her. She's so lucky to have someone like you who cares enough about her to work on healing the wounds she's living with." Show your inner child that you care for her by writing her a letter or poem acknowledging her pain. Help her feel seen and loved by validating the emotions she may feel about the unmet needs and wounds she has experienced.

_____

_____

_____

_____

_____

_____

_____

_____

_____

_____

_____

_____

_____

_____

_____

_____

_____

_____

HEALING YOUR SLEEP

Going to sleep means putting your defenses down, and survival mode wants you to stay alert and protected from threats at all times. To maintain that protection, a common trauma response is difficulty falling or staying asleep. You may also feel fatigued or low on energy, even after a full night of sleep, due to nightmares, nervous system dysregulation, or other disturbances. Healing your sleep is an important step in the trauma healing process, and creating a healthy and consistent sleep hygiene routine is a helpful way to work toward that healing.

Dear Me,

To help set myself up for success with sleep, this is what I want my sleep hygiene routine to look like.

I will not drink caffeine after _____, and I will stop using screens
                                       (time)

at _____. Instead of using screens, I'll _____, _____, or
     (time)

_____ before going to sleep. My sleep environment will
 (calming activities)

have _____ and _____ to create a calm and
                      (calming/comforting items)

comfortable space.

I'll get into bed to go to sleep between _____ and

_____ and wake up between
(times within one hour of each other)

_____ and _____, whenever I can,
                    (times within one hour of each other)

including on weekends. I'll wait until _____
                                   (at least one hour after waking)

to start using screens again. I understand how important sleep is for my

healing journey, and I'm excited to give myself the gift of improved sleep.

Love,

Me

SCREEN-FREE ZONE

We aren't meant to be exposed to media 24/7. We just aren't. The media, including many news outlets, social media sites, and podcasts, does its best to make you feel afraid, which keeps you hooked and coming back for more of its content. This means consuming media has the potential to activate your sympathetic nervous system (fight-or-flight mode).

Consuming media about events that affect a group of people you're part of can be a collective trauma experience, such as watching the news about a natural disaster in your area. You may also experience secondary trauma, which is when you learn about traumatic events that don't directly affect you. Because consuming media can actually cause trauma, limiting screen time is a helpful daily self-care practice to manage stress levels.

Choose one screen-free zone in your living space (such as your bedroom or kitchen). This will help you take a break from media at some point every day.

It may be helpful to list two or three activities that bring you joy, peace, or relaxation that you can use to replace media consumption, like reading or working on a creative project.

_____

_____

_____

_____

_____

_____

_____

_____

_____

_____

IF SOCIAL MEDIA LOOKED LIKE REAL LIFE

Social media can prompt lots of comparisons with the people and events we see. We're often comparing our full selves to a snippet of others' lives, however, and it's usually only their perfect snapshot that we get to see. Imagine how different social media would be if everyone were honest and vulnerable. Let's have a little fun with that!

In the space provided, practice using humor, creativity, and authenticity by writing funny social media posts. They can be based on real experiences, or not, and you don't have to post or share them with anyone unless you want to.

Example: *I woke up thirty minutes late, forgot to brush my teeth, and tripped over my cat on the way out the door—I'm on a roll this morning!*

_____

_____

_____

_____

_____

_____

_____

_____

_____

_____

_____

_____

_____

_____

_____

_____

_____

I will take care of myself now in all the ways I've always deserved to be cared for.

KEY TAKEAWAYS

Unhealthy coping skills and difficulty with self-care are common and understandable responses to trauma; learning to make room for and use healthy coping skills and self-care practices is an important part of the healing journey. You'll want to focus on areas such as understanding and valuing your needs, allowing yourself to rest, managing your stress well, getting to know your inner child, and healing your sleep. Practice patience and compassion with yourself as you slowly build new healthy coping skills and self-care practices.

- Traumatic experiences can affect your self-worth, which can lead to you feeling you're not worth taking care of.

- When you consistently put others first or otherwise ignore your needs, trauma healing can be more challenging, and you can get stuck in self-neglect.

- Know that it's okay and normal to have needs, and remind yourself of this as often as necessary.

- You can reparent yourself by treating your inner child in all the ways she wished to be treated and the ways you know she deserved to be treated.

- Self-care isn't just bubble baths. It is also embracing healthy habits around getting enough sleep, nourishing your body, and limiting your use of technology and social media.

FEELING SAFE IN YOUR BODY

Your body is your wisest resource. It knows how to protect you, and it knows how to heal. When you experience trauma, however, you become disconnected from your body, losing trust and feeling unsafe in your own skin. Your body may end up feeling like an uncomfortable and foreign place, which can be sad, scary, and confusing.

An important part of the healing process involves learning how to connect, trust, and listen to your body's wisdom again, or for the first time. This will not happen all at once. It will take time and lots of practice, so go easy on yourself as you start implementing the new tools and insights you'll learn in this section.

In the pages ahead, you'll explore the relationship between the body and trauma and learn how to increase body awareness. You'll take a look at how trauma affects body image and the unhealthy coping skills that can develop as a result, so you can start to befriend your body. Using the strategies you'll find in this section can help you continue to increase your awareness about and work toward nervous system regulation and balance, which are necessary steps in the trauma healing process. I hope you'll cultivate a feeling of safety in your body, so it can start to feel like home.

"The body...is where we experience most of our pain, pleasure, and joy, and where we process most of what happens to us. It is also where we do most of our healing."

—RESMAA MENAKEM

Priya's Story: Finding Balance in Her Mind and Body

Priya was an ambitious, self-aware, and funny young woman with a history of repeated traumatic experiences. In childhood, she experienced emotional and verbal abuse and witnessed physical abuse that was directed toward her siblings, and at school she was ostracized and bullied about her physical appearance.

This led to rebellious teen years and a habit of overworking herself to avoid the stress at home and the difficult emotions she felt. She started using other unhealthy coping skills (including cycles of restrictive eating and overexercising, linking her value to her achievements, and isolation) to help manage self-criticism, feelings of shame and guilt, perfectionism, and poor body image. Priya also struggled to form healthy relationships with herself and others.

Through therapy, she began to recognize these unhelpful patterns and establish healthy coping skills. Priya chose to go no-contact with her abusive parent. She also learned to better regulate her nervous system by giving herself permission to rest; paying attention to how people, places, and situations affect her stress levels; and developing a healthy relationship with her body. Priya began creating healthy relationships with others by being more vulnerable with safe people, setting healthy boundaries, and embracing opportunities to meet new people.

Although she was able to find balance with her eating and exercise habits and improve her body image, Priya's biggest challenges came with addressing self-compassion and acceptance. She continues to work on them so she can experience long-lasting change and continued post-traumatic growth.

TRAUMA ISN'T "ALL IN YOUR HEAD"

Trauma doesn't affect only your mind. It also affects your body in various ways that can leave a lasting impact. Somatic (bodily) symptoms that emerge after trauma and have no clear physical cause can be a sign of unprocessed emotions and/or trauma that are stuck in your body. This can look like chronic fatigue or frequent stomachaches that are not associated with any medical condition or the onset of an autoimmune disease following a traumatic event.

These somatic symptoms occur because of trauma's often long-term and overwhelming impact on the body's stress response system, which can lead to long-term health problems as it disrupts your body's functioning and ability to regulate stress.

Circle Yes for each somatic symptom and condition in the following list that you've experienced that **did not** have a clear physical cause and/or started following a traumatic event, and No for those you haven't experienced. This checklist is not a diagnostic tool, but rather, a guide to increase your awareness and understanding of the various ways trauma can affect your body.

1. **Chronic pain**
   Yes   No

2. **Chronic illness**
   Yes   No

3. **Chronic fatigue**
   Yes   No

4. **Sexual dysfunction**
   Yes   No

5. **Autoimmune disease**
   Yes   No

6. **Hormone imbalances**
   Yes   No

continued on next page

continued from previous page

7. **Gastrointestinal issues**

   Yes   No

8. **Vocal cord dysfunction**

   Yes   No

9. **Short, shallow breathing**

   Yes   No

10. **Depressed immune system**

    Yes   No

11. **Frequent headaches or migraines**

    Yes   No

12. **Chronic muscle tension or soreness**

    Yes   No

13. **Heightened or lack of sensation in an area of the body**

    Yes   No

CREATING A CALMING ENVIRONMENT

Do you notice you feel calmer when your living space is clean versus when it's dirty or unorganized? Or maybe you notice you feel more at peace around certain people than you do around others. Like plants, animals, and all living things, we are affected by our environment, and that means our nervous systems are affected as well. List up to eight ways you can help yourself feel safe, connected, and grounded in your environment at home, backyard, work, or another important space (for example, keep it clean, create a calming area in your home or yard).

_____

_____

_____

_____

_____

_____

_____

_____

_____

_____

_____

_____

_____

_____

_____

_____

LEARNING TO LISTEN TO AND TRUST BODILY SENSATIONS

Trauma is stored in your mind and body; it's stored in your sensory memory, nervous system, physical sensations, reflexes, and posture. Building awareness of the sensations and tension throughout your body will help you feel more connected to, and therefore safer in, your body. By tuning in to your body, you can also learn to listen to and trust your body's sensations, rather than be closed off to or scared of them.

Go online and search for a five- to ten-minute guided progressive muscle relaxation video on a site such as YouTube. If you use an app such as Headspace, you can search there, too. Set aside some quiet time for yourself and use the video to do a guided progressive muscle relaxation exercise.

Pay close attention to the sensations throughout your body as you complete it. When you're finished, circle the words that most closely describe the physical sensations you noticed while completing the progressive muscle relaxation. Building your somatic vocabulary can be incredibly helpful in increasing awareness of your experience and using your body as a resource on your healing journey.

Achy	Damp	Numb	Tense
Burning	Empty	Prickly	Tight
Clenched	Fluttery	Radiating	Tingly
Constricted	Heavy	Sharp	Trembling
Cool	Light	Stiff	Vibrating
			Warm

CULTIVATING CONNECTION IN THE BODY

Becoming disconnected from your emotions and your body is an extremely common adaptive response that develops as protection from significant mental, emotional, or physical pain and allows you to continue living and surviving. This disconnection is also known as *dissociation* (when some aspects of how we function are removed from conscious awareness). Dissociation is a protective avoidance strategy that can include daydreaming, minimization (*It could've been worse*), numbness, and/or not remembering certain blocks of time. It often continues after the traumatic event has ended, until you feel safe enough to learn new ways of coping and connecting.

When it persists after the danger has passed, it can interfere with your healing process by blocking you from connecting with yourself, your body, and the present moment. Here are two practical somatic exercises you can use to help you cultivate connection within your body by safely processing the emotions stored there:

1. **Stand or sit and let your whole body shake loosely for one to two minutes. Focus on the tension being released in different parts of your body. Slow down gradually, stop, and notice how your body feels.**
   (*Suggested uses: to ease anxiety, irritation, or frustration*)

2. **Place your right hand on your left shoulder and your left hand on your right shoulder, like you're giving yourself a hug. Alternate tapping on each shoulder in a slow, rhythmic pattern. If you want, you can also gently rock back and forth or sway from side to side.**
   (*Suggested uses: to ease sadness, grief, or feeling overwhelmed*)

Most people experience some kind of dissociation at some point in their lives. Dissociative symptoms that last a long time or are especially intense and significantly affect your life may be a sign of a dissociative disorder. If you think you may be experiencing this, consult with a therapist who can help.

YOUR SELF-CONNECTION LIST

In response to stress or a perceived threat, you can experience fight, flight, freeze, or fawn responses. Your response may differ depending on the situation, or you may lean toward certain responses over others. In general, women may be more likely than men to use the fawn response, possibly because women tend to be raised to be caretakers and prioritize others' needs above their own.

Each response can involve aspects of disconnection. For example, freeze involves numbness, while fawn involves disconnecting from your bodily sensations to cut yourself off from your needs.

Being able to find connection within yourself is important for many reasons, and self-care, self-compassion, and self-acceptance can increase self-connection. Some signs you're gaining self-connection are feeling and processing your emotions, recognizing and meeting your needs, a greater sense of inner peace, and building a kinder, more loving relationship with yourself.

Use the space here to reflect on strategies, activities, and resources you have used or want to try to create a greater sense of connection within yourself.

1. Ways I can embrace self-care:

_____

_____

2. Ways I can embrace self-compassion:

_____

_____

3. Ways I can embrace self-acceptance:

_____

_____

PERMISSION TO SLOW DOWN

A common myth about nervous system regulation is that being regulated means being perfectly behaved or completely calm all the time. If this were the case, you'd be a robot, not a human. Instead, regulating your nervous system expands your capacity to feel all your emotions and to be with whatever experience is happening in your body, and it increases your ability to return to a calm state after experiencing life's challenges. Cultivating these responses will help you move out of survival mode.

It's normal to experience life's challenges and the full range of emotions, especially when we live in a society that prioritizes productivity and achievement. It's not uncommon to feel shame about slowing down or resting, when there is seemingly constant pressure to be busy and rushed. You may also feel this shame because of internalized beliefs about your worth being tied to productivity. But as we're learning throughout this book, slowing down and managing your sense of being overwhelmed are necessary steps for healing.

1. How can you encourage yourself to slow down and give yourself permission to do so without guilt?

_____

_____

2. List up to six ways you can slow down (that is, set boundaries to avoid overcommitting yourself).

_____

_____

_____

_____

_____

_____

YOUR BODY REMEMBERS WHAT YOUR MIND DOESN'T

I've worked with clients who seem to struggle around the same time each year without any noticeable cause, until we realize this is likely due to a traumatic event they experienced during that time in the past; their body is remembering even if their mind is not. This is one example of how traumatic memories are stored differently than other memories. They're stored beyond your conscious mind, in the nonverbal and emotional parts of your mind and directly in your body. This is why your body can often reveal more than your words can, which makes somatic work so important for trauma healing.

One somatic practice is called *tapping,* or *emotional freedom technique* (EFT). Gently tapping on specific acupressure points on your body sends calming signals to your brain and helps balance your nervous system. You can use it whenever you're triggered by something or feeling emotional distress, and it can also be used regularly for trauma healing by tapping as you focus on a traumatic memory or emotion. You're not trying to get rid of the memory or emotion, but rather, you want to change how you respond to it: with self-compassion and less reactivity. Try this tapping exercise:

Choose one mildly distressing memory to focus on. Rate the intensity of the memory from 0 to 10: _____. Acknowledge the memory, while accepting yourself fully.

Now you are going to use firm but gentle pressure to tap each of the following points of your body about five times.

On the right side of your body, use your left middle and index fingers together to tap the:

1. Outer side of your right hand (the pinkie finger side)
2. Inner point of the eyebrow
3. Outer side of the eye
4. Under the eye
5. Under the nose

6. Under the mouth (above the chin)
7. Collarbone
8. Under the arm (near the ribs)
9. Top of the head

Repeat on the left side of your body, using your right middle and index fingers together to tap those locations.

Rate the intensity of the memory again from 0 to 10: _____. If the intensity is still higher than you'd like, repeat again as needed until the intensity decreases.

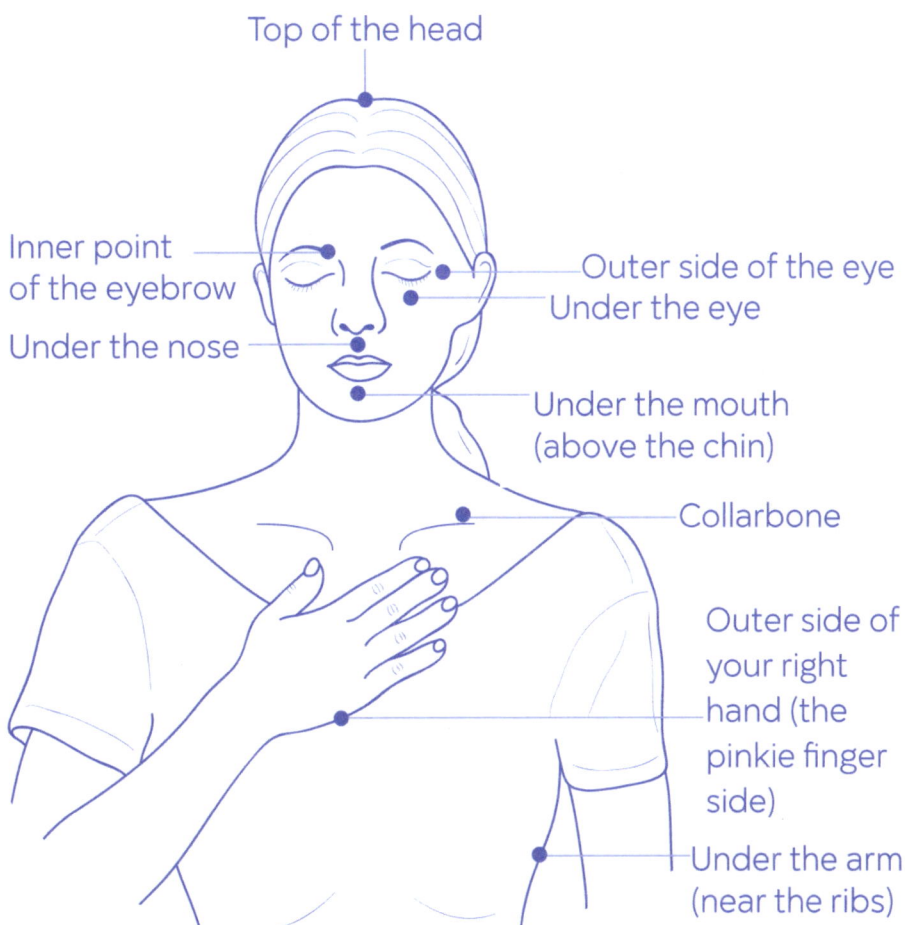

Top of the head

Inner point of the eyebrow

Outer side of the eye
Under the eye

Under the nose

Under the mouth (above the chin)

Collarbone

Outer side of your right hand (the pinkie finger side)

Under the arm (near the ribs)

REFRAMING BODY IMAGE MESSAGES

"Your body should be this size." "You shouldn't eat that." "You're only attractive if you look like this." You've probably heard messages or had thoughts like these at some point in your life. The implicit and explicit messages you receive from family, culture, and media about your body can be damaging.

The unrealistic standards to which we, as women, are often held (starting at a young age), and the pressure to meet those standards can cause unhealthy relationships with food and your body. These messages and standards also can be harmful to your mental and physical health, and they can lead to unhealthy coping skills such as overexercising, disordered eating (such as restrictive or emotional eating patterns) or eating disorders (such as anorexia or bulimia nervosa), and self-harm.

Reflect on any unhelpful thoughts and beliefs you have around your body and body image and where they came from (for example, family, friends, culture, or media). Then practice challenging the unhelpful messages you've received by reframing them as positive or neutral statements. If you're feeling stuck about reframing them, think about what messages you wish you had received about your body and body image.

UNHELPFUL THOUGHT OR BELIEF	WHERE IT CAME FROM	REFRAMED MESSAGE
Only certain types of bodies are okay.	*Culture and media*	*All body types, shapes, colors, and abilities are beautiful.*

BODY IMAGE RECOVERY

Women are sometimes taught that a violation of their body is somehow their fault (it's absolutely not!). Shame, self-criticism, and disconnection from your body are often the result. Disconnection can cause a distorted body image, when you feel as if your body is not part of yourself (that is, feeling as if you're outside of your body), and shame and self-criticism can be a source of harsh judgments about your body.

1. Reflect on any shame, self-criticism, or disconnection that is tied to your body image. How do these show up in your life?

   _____

   _____

   _____

2. When are each of these feelings most likely to show up (for example, when you are deciding whether to have dessert)?

   _____

   _____

   _____

3. What does each feeling need to be heard, seen, validated, and cared for? For example, your shame may need to hear that you acknowledge it and thank it for protecting you from deeper pain, but now you want to cope using self-compassion instead.

   _____

   _____

   _____

TREAT YOUR BODY LIKE A GOOD FRIEND

Your body deserves your unconditional love and kindness. I know, easier said than done. But one way you can begin to befriend your body is by using self-compassion for your body to shift your focus away from your physical appearance.

When your focus is on your physical appearance, your feelings about your body are very susceptible to change, depending on the day, feedback from others, and many other factors. For example, you feel great about how you look in a new outfit, but when someone makes an offhand comment about it, your self-esteem takes an immediate dip and you no longer feel good about your appearance.

By shifting your focus to compassion for your body, you're more likely to have a strong and steady stream of gratitude, love, and acceptance for this precious vessel that keeps you alive. These feelings can withstand day-to-day changes in your circumstances.

On the following page, draw an outline of your body as you see it. Fill it in with colors and images that elicit feelings of compassion, love, and gratitude. You might pay extra attention to areas of your body that you have particular difficulty accepting or that experience more frequent or intense discomfort. Next, fill in the area around this image with affirmations to use when body-shaming thoughts come into your mind, such as *I appreciate everything my body does for me* and *My body deserves my love and respect.*

SCANNING FOR STRENGTH

Let's use a body scan to practice connecting to your body without judgment. This particular body scan will also help you identify areas of your body that are sources of strength you can use as a resource during challenging times. Although you'll ask if each area of your body has strength, be mindful not to label any area as good or bad, better or worse.

1. Get comfortable, close your eyes or soften your gaze, and take three slow, deep breaths.
2. Shift your focus to your feet and ask yourself, *Is there strength in this area?*
3. If the answer is no, begin to shift your focus to the next area of your body.
4. If the answer is yes, remain focused here for a few moments, connecting more deeply and experiencing the strength the area is providing. Remember, you can connect with this strength whenever you need it.
5. Slowly move up your body from one area to the next (feet, lower legs, upper legs, hips, and so on) until you reach your head.
6. You may choose which areas to focus on, and it's okay to stop at or skip certain areas that don't feel safe or comfortable to connect with.
7. Notice each area with calm awareness and curiosity. And ask each one, "Is there strength in this area?"
8. When you have completed the body scan, open your eyes and bring your focus back to your surroundings.

RECLAIMING CONTROL AND CHOICE

Practicing yoga can help you safely reconnect with your body, reduce stress, develop a sense of acceptance and presence, and establish a sense of wholeness within yourself. It can also help increase your confidence and self-trust and, when done in a class, build a strong sense of community. Yoga can be helpful for survivors of any kind of trauma, and it may be especially helpful for survivors of sexual trauma to reclaim a sense of control and choice over their body.

For this practice, you'll do the Mountain Pose, a foundational and empowering yoga pose. This practice is not about pushing your limits, so make any adjustments you need for your comfort and safety. You might consider doing this in a safe space outdoors, for the added benefits of nervous system regulation that occur with both gentle physical move-ment and spending time in nature.

1. Stand with your big toes touching and your heels slightly apart.
2. Lift and spread your toes and then lower them back to the floor.
3. Align your head, shoulders, hips, and ankles in a straight line.
4. Relax your arms by your sides with your palms facing forward.
5. Imagine there's a string on the top of your head pulling your body upward, keeping your neck long and straightening your entire body.
6. Embrace the power and strength you feel in your body and heart.
7. Breathe deeply and hold this position for one to two minutes (if you can).
8. Continue breathing as you gently release this pose.

DEAR BODY

With all the knowledge and insights you've gained throughout this section, complete this letter by filling in the blanks to express your newfound or renewed gratitude and love for your body.

Dear Body,

You've been here protecting me all this time. I understand, or I'm beginning to understand, just how wise you are and how important you are for my healing journey. I appreciate everything you do, including how you function and how you look, and I love how _____ _____. Thank you for always taking care of me and keeping me safe. I haven't always treated you with care, but I will treat you with love and care now by _____.

I trust you to be a safe place for me to reconnect with you. Some of my favorite ways to connect with you are _____ _____. I'm thankful for the wisdom of my nervous system to adjust, and I've learned to help find the balance and flow of it by _____ _____. I promise to do my best to treat you with love, kindness, and _____ _____. You're starting to feel like home to me, and I'm honored that you're my _____ body.

With love and care,

_____(your name)

I trust my body to be a place of safety and connection.

KEY TAKEAWAYS

Trauma affects not only your mind but also your body. Because your body is your wisest resource, it makes sense that healing through your body is an important aspect of your trauma healing journey. This can mean gaining awareness, trust, safety, and connection in your body, which you can work toward by learning how to regulate and balance your nervous system and treating your body with compassion.

- Your body knows how to protect you, and it knows how to heal. But through traumatic experiences, you may have become disconnected from your body, losing trust and no longer feeling safe in it.

- Somatic symptoms with no clear physical cause and/or that develop after a traumatic event can be a sign of unprocessed emotions and/or trauma stuck in your body.

- Becoming disconnected from your emotions and your body is an extremely adaptive response that develops as protection from significant mental, emotional, or physical pain and allows you to continue living and surviving. But when this disconnection persists after the danger has passed, it can interfere with your healing process by blocking you from connecting with yourself, your body, and the present moment.

- Regulating your nervous system expands your capacity to feel all your emotions and to be with whatever experience is happening in your body. It also increases your ability to return to a calm state after experiencing life's challenges.

BUILDING SELF-LOVE

Along with its impact on your relationships with others, trauma can have negative effects on the most important relationship you'll ever have—your relationship with yourself. Trauma disconnects you from yourself and destabilizes your sense of self, your self-beliefs, and your values. These distorted views of self often lead to shame and low self-worth, and have a negative effect on your relationships with yourself and others and how you move through the world. Building self-love can be a transformational step for trauma survivors, and it will help you move forward on your healing journey.

The information and strategies you learned in the other sections of this book, such as acknowledging your emotions and responding to your needs with compassion, will help you create a safe relationship with yourself. This section will take you on a deeper dive into building self-worth and restoring a safe and healthy relationship with yourself. You'll explore and heal the negative self-concepts and self-limiting beliefs that can form as a result of trauma. You'll also discover how to accept all parts of yourself, build self-trust, and use practical techniques to embrace self-love in your everyday life. I'm so excited to walk alongside you on this important step of your journey!

"This revolutionary act of treating ourselves tenderly can begin to undo the aversive messages of a lifetime."
—TARA BRACH

Maya's Story: Self-Love Set Her Free

Maya was in a long-term relationship with a partner who was unfaithful to her and engaged in emotionally abusive behaviors. As a result, Maya experienced heightened anxiety and bouts of depression, and her self-worth was completely broken down. She kept cycling though emotional high highs and very low lows, and she started to believe the critical things her partner said about her.

Although there were times when Maya could recognize that she deserved to be treated better, those times were short-lived because the harsh self-talk and limiting beliefs would quickly make their return. When she talked about leaving, her partner declared that Maya would never be able to find anyone else who would love her, and she believed that. Ultimately, Maya felt inadequate, flawed, and worthless.

Maya remained in therapy, working on anxiety and mood management, nervous system regulation, and building her self-worth. Finally, she made the choice to break up with her partner for good. She grieved the relationship and was kind to herself in acknowledging that breakups are hard no matter the circumstances. She understood that her newfound self-love and improved self-worth helped her break free from that abusive relationship and see hope on the other side. She also recognized that the breakup was not the end point of her healing journey, and she continued to grow in her self-love.

UNDERSTANDING YOUR SELF-CONCEPTS

Have you ever asked yourself *Who am I?* Well, exploring your self-concept can help answer that question. *Self-concept* refers to your overall perception of yourself; it includes your beliefs about yourself, as well as your self-esteem and self-identity. It's a broad picture of who you are, shaped by experiences, social interactions, and self-evaluations, and it becomes the lens through which you see yourself.

Your self-concept is very vulnerable to being affected by trauma, and a number of unhealthy self-concepts can emerge in the wake of traumatic experiences. This happens because trauma disrupts your sense of safety, control, trust, shame, and self-worth, which can distort your view of yourself, make it difficult to define who you are outside of the traumatic experience(s), and lead to you carrying persistent negative core beliefs about yourself.

On the word wall here are common self-concepts that can develop from trauma. Color in the bricks on the wall for the self-concepts you relate to. Choose colors that represent each self-concept for you. If other words come to mind (such as *hopeless*, *helpless*, or *unkind*), you can write those down and color them in on the blank bricks. View each brick through a lens of self-compassion and understanding.

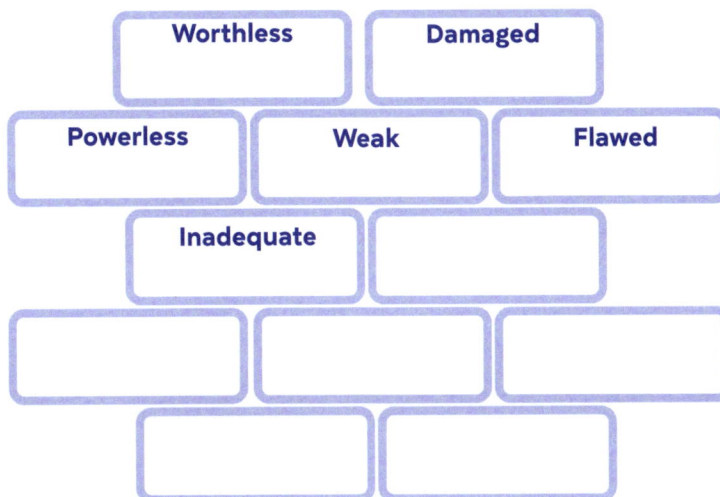

Worthless	Damaged

Powerless	Weak	Flawed

Inadequate	

RESTORING YOUR SENSE OF SELF

Trauma can create a significant change in your self-concept by causing you to question your sense of self, your ability to trust yourself, your values, and your ability to care for yourself. You may even feel as if the person you were before the trauma is a stranger to you now. Although it may not seem like it yet, you can restore your self-concept, and I'm here to help guide you toward that.

1. Choose one challenging experience you've had that feels tolerable to think about (for example, you didn't make a sports team or you experienced the breakup of a relationship).

_____

_____

_____

_____

2. How did your view of yourself, your self-beliefs, your values, or your self-worth change after that experience?

_____

_____

_____

3. How have you been able to rebuild your self-concept since then? If you haven't yet, that's okay. You'll learn strategies to help throughout this section.

_____

_____

_____

MAY YOU LOVE YOURSELF

Loving-kindness (or metta) meditation began in Buddhist practice thousands of years ago. It can help you build your self-love and self-worth by reducing self-criticism and strengthening self-kindness and acceptance. Research has shown that consistent use of a loving-kindness meditation can effectively reduce trauma symptoms and increase self-compassion. Try practicing this meditation every day for one week. At the end of the week, reflect on any changes in your feelings of self-love, kindness, and acceptance.

Make yourself comfortable, close your eyes or soften your gaze, or stand in front of a mirror with your eyes open. Take a few deep breaths, and repeat silently to yourself:

I am thankful for this body.

I am thankful for this mind.

I am thankful for this spirit.

I am doing the best I can in life.

May my body, mind, and spirit be healthy.

May my body, mind, and spirit be safe from outside dangers.

May my body, mind, and spirit be safe from inside dangers.

May my body, mind, and spirit be honored and loved.

May I honor myself.

May I love myself.

Stay with these intentions for a few moments. When you're ready, open your eyes and bring your focus back to your surroundings.

GET TO KNOW YOUR PROTECTOR PARTS

We have many different aspects of our personalities within ourselves. In Internal Family Systems (IFS) therapy, these are referred to as *parts*.

Protector parts look out for your safety and survival and work hard to shield you from pain. When your Protectors are responding to trauma, they're often trying to get your unmet needs met while you are feeling fear, shame, a wounded self-concept, and/or low self-worth. For example, your People Pleaser part tries to get the love and acceptance it longs for by putting others first and not using your voice. Even though other parts of you may know there are better ways to get those needs met, the People Pleaser has done its best with the resources it has.

In the following table, you'll find names and descriptions of some Protector parts. Think about which Protectors most resonate with you. On the shield, write your thoughts, limiting beliefs, or behaviors that are related to those Protector parts. The shield represents your acknowledgment of their role in protecting and keeping you safe, and the superwoman is a reminder that you're capable and strong, and you can form a healthy relationship with your Protectors now.

PROTECTOR PART	DESCRIPTION
Avoider	Numbs or distracts you to avoid facing difficult emotions and situations
Inner Critic	Believes using shame and self-blame will protect you from rejection and other pain
Overachiever	Believes your worth depends on your accomplishments and pushes you to do more
People Pleaser	Suppresses your needs and avoids conflict to focus on gaining acceptance
Perfectionist	Sets unattainable standards and believes you must be perfect to be accepted
Procrastinator	Avoids any task or decision that could lead to rejection, failure, or criticism
Self-Saboteur	Believes it's safer to not have good things, to avoid the pain of losing a good thing

ACCEPTING ALL YOUR PARTS

All parts of you are good and helpful, even if it doesn't always feel that way. Every part has been needed and had a purpose in helping you survive. You don't need to get rid of any of your parts; rather, get to know and accept each of them. When you're able to do this, your parts feel much lighter and those that have been affected by trauma can find a new purpose (for example, the inner critic becomes the inner cheer-leader). With this imagery exercise, you'll get to know one of your parts more deeply and begin to accept it.

1. Make yourself comfortable, close your eyes or soften your gaze, and take three slow, deep breaths.
2. Identify a part of you that you have trouble accepting, such as a Procrastinator part or an Angry part. (Try to choose a part that isn't deeply connected to your trauma. If you do so unknowingly, pause and come back to this practice later to complete it using a different part.)
3. Imagine what this part looks like, feels like, and sounds like. (It might look/feel/sound like you, or some version of you, or like an animal, object, shape, or color.)
4. Ask what purpose this part has served for you.
5. Thank it for serving its purpose.
6. Consider how can you shift your relationship to this part.
7. Start to direct feelings of acceptance toward this part and ask it what it needs from you. Let it know that you hear it and care for it.
8. Reflect on what might become this part's new purpose.
9. Imagine providing this part strength and confidence to move toward its new purpose.
10. Take a few deep breaths and reflect on how you feel toward this part now.

EXPLORING SELF-LIMITING BELIEFS

Self-limiting beliefs are born from a negative or wounded self-concept; they are the specific ideas you hold about your confidence and capabilities within that self-concept. For example, the self-limiting belief *I can't be fixed* might stem from the self-concept that you are "damaged." Increasing your awareness of your self-limiting beliefs can help reveal how they've become woven into your choices, behaviors, emotions, and relationships.

1. Describe one scenario where your self-limiting beliefs tend to show up (such as a job interview, speaking up for yourself, or meeting a new person).

    _____

    _____

    _____

    _____

2. What self-limiting belief(s) tend to come up in this scenario? (For more self-limiting belief examples, see the next exercise.)

    _____

    _____

    _____

    _____

3. How are these limiting beliefs affecting your choices, behaviors, emotions, or relationships in this scenario?

    _____

    _____

    _____

    _____

MAKE YOUR MIND A SAFE PLACE

Self-limiting beliefs can be tricky to overcome because they often arise from past situations in which they *were* true or *felt* true. For example:

1. **Were true:** Someone who experienced childhood trauma was likely powerless to stop or leave the situation, so they now operate as if they're powerless, even though that's no longer true.
2. **Felt true:** Someone who was repeatedly told they were too sensitive or dramatic might have internalized that judgment, so now they believe they're too much, even though that was never true.

Understanding this concept can help you bring more compassion to your experience with self-limiting beliefs. From the following list, circle three beliefs that most resonate with you.

I can't do anything right.	*I don't matter.*
I'll never succeed.	*I'm not valuable.*
No one likes me.	*I'm unlovable.*
I don't deserve good things.	*I'm not capable.*
I'm broken.	*I'm too much.*
I'm not enough.	*I'm a bad person.*

Now, challenge each belief you circled. For example, to challenge *I'm not enough*, you might reframe this as *I'm enough just as I am*.

1. _____

2. _____

3. _____

Say the first self-limiting belief in your head or aloud, and notice where you feel the belief in your body. Gently touch this place, and provide it with love while repeating your new, reframed belief. Repeat with the next two beliefs, and repeat this exercise as often as needed.

REMEMBER YOUR CAPABILITIES

Negative thoughts and self-limiting beliefs can make it difficult to recognize or remember all the things you are really good at. Write about three things that have gone well this week, including things both big and small. Take a moment to reflect on and write down what it is about you that enabled you to accomplish these things (for example, you set a boundary that enabled you to accomplish a personal goal). Allow yourself to sit with this reflection, soaking in how it feels to accept your accomplishments, strengths, and capabilities.

1. _____

_____

_____

_____

2. _____

_____

_____

_____

_____

3. _____

_____

_____

_____

_____

_____

YOU DESERVE TO BE SEEN AND HEARD

If you feel uncomfortable being seen, taking up space, or speaking up for yourself, you're not alone. There are many possible reasons for this discomfort. For women, it can be because society has often made us feel responsible for making others comfortable, so we're less likely to speak up for ourselves or make our needs and desires known.

For trauma survivors, it may be because you've been in situations where being seen or speaking up wasn't safe, so you learned to stay quiet to protect yourself. Whatever the reason is for you, I want you to know that you deserve to be seen, be heard, and take up space in this world.

Use the ideas that follow to gently practice being seen, being heard, and taking up space. Check off which ones would be most helpful for you, and write down other ideas you can think of in the spaces provided.

☐ Accept compliments by saying "Thank you" rather than minimizing or deflecting them.

☐ Let your restaurant server know when there's a mistake with your order.

☐ Try to stop using the word "just" unnecessarily (for example, "I just feel like…" becomes "I feel…").

☐ _____
_____

☐ _____
_____

☐ _____
_____

☐ _____
_____

KEEP YOUR PROMISES TO YOURSELF

With the emotions (such as fear and anxiety) and the negative self-perceptions (such as limiting beliefs and wounded self-concepts) that can come from trauma, it makes sense that you may have trouble trusting yourself. Those emotions and negative perceptions make it difficult to trust your judgments, decisions, and abilities.

Just as we tend to trust others who keep their promises and show up for us, by consistently showing up for and keeping promises you make to yourself you will teach yourself that you are a safe and trusted person.

Check off each promise you'd like to make to yourself. Choose one to start, and make an action plan for how you'll follow through on it.

To really lock in these promises, try using a hand sign when you think about your promises; you might cross your middle finger over your index finger or give yourself a pinkie promise. Or write them down or say them aloud to yourself.

Each day, I will…

☐ *Practice compassionate self-talk*

☐ *Make space to safely process my emotions*

☐ *Do something I enjoy*

☐ *Set aside time for rest*

☐ *Show love to my body with gentle movement*

☐ Other: _____

☐ Other: _____

☐ Other: _____

My action plan for follow-through:

1. _____
   _____

2. _____
   _____

3. _____
   _____

SMALL STEPS TO HEALING

Self-love is important for everyone; it can be especially important for trauma survivors. Building self-love can be incredibly helpful in mending the wounded self-image, self-beliefs, and self-worth that can come from trauma. But building self-love is not a quick process, and it requires patience. With every small step you take, such as each time you use compassionate self-talk or speak up for yourself, you plant a seed to help your self-love grow.

1. How can you be patient with yourself and give yourself grace throughout your healing journey?

_____

_____

_____

_____

2. Write down what words of support you would offer a friend on their healing journey.

_____

_____

_____

_____

3. How can you apply those same words or actions to supporting yourself?

_____

_____

_____

_____

PAST AND PRESENT VALUES

Exploring your values can help strengthen your sense of self and challenge self-limiting beliefs. This exercise will help you do that by uncovering values that are important to you now. It can be really interesting and helpful to learn where your values came from and how your current values compare to those you grew up with. You'll choose one value to focus on, but you can repeat this exercise as many times as you'd like with other values.

First, choose one value you'd like to explore. Some ideas include achievement, authenticity, equality, freedom, happiness, health, leisure, respect, security, tradition, trust, and truth.

Reflect on how this value was prioritized, expressed, or rejected in the past with your family of origin (that is, your primary caregivers and other immediate family members), your larger community and culture (close friends, your spiritual community, your ethnic group), and within yourself today.

Value: _____

FAMILY OF ORIGIN	COMMUNITY AND CULTURE	SELF TODAY

COMPLETING THE SELF-LOVE PUZZLE

Sometimes when you feel unworthy, you focus on how you can care for or prove yourself to others, rather than on taking care of yourself. One reason you might do this is because it allows you to mask feelings of unworthiness. Instead of uncovering the true roots and emotions of the unworthiness, you see your worth in caring for others. While it's absolutely valid to see value in caring for others, if you don't also see value in caring for yourself, you're missing an important piece of the self-love puzzle.

What emotions come up for you when you think about putting yourself first? List some affirmations to use when you notice that you're prioritizing others above yourself. For example, *My needs are important and worth getting met* or *Putting myself first is not selfish.*

_____

_____

_____

_____

_____

_____

_____

_____

_____

_____

_____

_____

_____

_____

GROWING YOUR SELF-LOVE

As you continue your healing journey, you will likely gradually find it easier to release self-limiting beliefs and embrace the positive aspects of yourself you may have lost sight of. In the leaves of the plants pictured below, write down positive beliefs or traits you already possess or wish to nurture as you heal. These may be things such as being resilient, strong, honest, fair, creative, resourceful, or smart—whatever comes to mind. Then, alongside the lines coming out of the watering can, write down the ways you will nourish these positive things about yourself. This might be with self-love, self-compassion, positive self-talk, self-care, acceptance, patience, being in community with others, or whatever else you can think of.

I give myself the love and acceptance I need.

KEY TAKEAWAYS

Trauma has a significant impact on self-concept, beliefs, values, and worth, and restoring these important aspects of self is essential to your healing journey. You can focus on restoring and building your self-love while on your healing journey by getting to know and accepting all parts of yourself, understanding and challenging your self-limiting beliefs, increasing self-trust, exploring your values, and practicing compassionate self-talk. Building self-love takes time and patience; remember to give yourself grace along the way.

- Trauma can create significant changes in your ideas about yourself by causing you to question your sense of self, your ability to trust yourself, your values, and your belief in yourself.

- Protector parts are looking out for your safety and survival and working hard to shield you from pain. You can form a healthier relationship with them.

- Increasing awareness of your self-limiting beliefs can help reveal how they've become woven into your choices, behaviors, emotions, and relationships.

- I want you to know that you deserve to be seen, be heard, and take up space in this world.

- Every small step you take is planting a seed to help your self-love grow.

SECTION 8
CREATING HEALTHY RELATIONSHIPS

Trauma deeply affects your relationships. It can show up in the relationship you have with your goals, with your money, or in just about any area of life. But it is especially present in your relationships with other people.

Imagine having relationships where you feel safe and calm, where you can trust that you'll be treated well mentally, physically, and emotionally, accepted for who you are, and can confidently put your guard down. Sounds pretty great, right? These relationships can feel out of reach for trauma survivors, but they are possible for you through healing and connecting with safe and supportive people.

In this section, we're going to explore how trauma may be showing up in your relationships and your attachment style, and how you can move out of relationship patterns meant to protect yourself and toward connection.

Through the healing process, you'll learn how to create healthier relationships. An important bonus is that engaging in and learning to trust these bonds will foster even more healing.

Another important part of this section is identifying your safe people and learning how to build healthy and rewarding relationships. My hope is that you'll finish this section with more awareness and relationship skills, and more hope for having meaningful bonds in your life.

"Your connectedness to other people is so key to buffering any current stressor—and to healing from past trauma. Being with people who are present, supportive, and nurturing. Belonging."
—TARA BRACH

Maria's Story: Finding Freedom from Unhealthy Patterns

Maria had emotionally immature parents who often exploded with anger, criticized her, did not take responsibility for their mistakes or try to mend them, and met her needs inconsistently or not at all. As a result, she grew up with a lot of fear and confusion. These early relationships with her parents created a road map for her future relationships. She struggled to see her worth, identify and voice her needs, and feel safe in relationships.

Familiar patterns can feel comfortable and safe, even when they aren't, and Maria had a long cycle of unhealthy relationships with inconsistent, emotionally unavailable, and otherwise unhealthy partners that felt similar to her relationship with her parents.

In therapy, Maria was able to experience a safe relationship with her therapist, which enabled her to let her guard down, open up about her past, and recognize the unhealthy relationship patterns she had been repeating. Gradually, Maria was able to open herself up to being more vulnerable, reparenting herself, and learning healthy relationship skills, such as setting healthy boundaries and open communication. She learned to safely connect with herself and others and to stop repeating the patterns of her past. Her family relationships are still challenging, but she has built stronger friendships and disrupted the cycle of unhealthy romantic partners.

Although it wasn't easy at first because her mind and body weren't yet sure how to accept a loving relationship that comes without chaos, she's now in a long-term, healthy relationship with a partner who treats her the way she has always deserved to be treated.

HOW TRAUMA AFFECTS RELATIONSHIPS

When we understand that trauma shuts down the social part of our brain, it makes sense that it causes social disconnection and can have a profound impact on relationships. Trauma may show up more often or in different ways in different relationships, but it can show up in any relationship you have: with family, friends, romantic partners, work colleagues, school peers, total strangers, and everyone else, including your therapist.

Here are some common ways trauma can show up in relationships. Reflect on your relationships and circle the qualities you tend to exhibit in them. Remember to give yourself grace and compassion for any qualities you circle; these are all common trauma responses, and you can heal from them.

Difficulty trusting others

Difficulty/discomfort with intimacy

Tendency to isolate

Relationships feel unsafe

Fear of abandonment or rejection

Self-sabotaging behavior

Avoiding conflict or being overly confrontational

Difficulty setting boundaries (for example, saying yes when you mean no)

Losing yourself in other people

Responding with defensiveness

Difficulty asking for or accepting help

Controlling behavior (for example, manipulation or unhealthy jealousy)

Tolerating unhealthy relationships

People-pleasing and/or codependency (such as putting others' needs before your own)

YOUR EARLY BONDS

Our early environments, experiences, and attachments have deep-rooted effects on us that can persist into adulthood, until we take a look at them and choose to heal and unlearn unhelpful patterns. Exploring your early relationships can help you better understand your current relationships, attachment styles, and attachment wounds.

1. How would you describe your childhood relationship with your caregivers and your observations of your caregivers' relationships with others?

   _____

   _____

   _____

   _____

   _____

   _____

   _____

2. In what ways do your adult relationships mirror these relationships?

   _____

   _____

   _____

   _____

   _____

   _____

   _____

IDENTIFYING YOUR ATTACHMENT STYLE

Your attachment style is initially shaped by the attachments you have with your primary caregiver(s) and childhood events, and it may change depending on your adult relationships. We tend to lean toward one attachment style, but we can have traits from more than one. Attachment styles can differ in different relationships, as well, such as those with a parent, partner, or friend.

Attachment styles can change, and it can also be difficult to pinpoint which style(s) you currently experience in your relationships. Still, understanding your attachment style is beneficial because it helps you recognize patterns in how you behave in relationships, understand where those patterns may come from, and identify areas of growth that will enable you to work toward building healthier and more secure relationships with others.

Let's get to know the different attachment styles and where some of your most important relationships currently fall within those styles.

Anxious Attachment

Typical origin: a childhood environment or important adult relationship that was unpredictable and inconsistent. As an adult it may show up as:

- Having a strong desire to be close to others

- Worrying excessively about the stability of relationships

- Fearing abandonment

Avoidant

Typical origin: a childhood environment or important adult relationship that involved neglect or rejection. As an adult this may show up as:

- Often valuing independence over intimacy

- Being uncomfortable with emotions and conflict

- Fearing vulnerability or commitment

Disorganized

Typical origin: a childhood environment or important adult relationship that was scary. As an adult it may show up as:

- Being highly emotionally dysregulated, with sudden shifts in mood

- Being suspicious of relationships and viewing them as unsafe

- Having characteristics of anxious and avoidant styles

Secure

Typical origin: a childhood environment or healing through important adult relationships that are predictable, loving, and responsive to your basic needs. As an adult this may show up as:

- Viewing other people and the world as generally safe

- Being open to connection

- Being able to handle and resolve conflict

Based on these descriptions, which attachment style(s) do you identify with? Consider different relationships you have and how your attachment style plays out in the following:

1. With a romantic partner: _____
2. With a parent: _____
3. With a work colleague: _____
4. With a friend: _____
5. With a stranger: _____

The good news is that you can develop secure attachment with safe people, no matter what experiences or attachment wounds you've had in the past. The exercises in the pages ahead will help you move toward greater security.

To learn more about attachment styles, I recommend working with a therapist and/or utilizing resources like the Diane Poole Heller book *The Power of Attachment.*

MAKING SMALL AND SAFE CONNECTIONS

When family members, intimate partners, or friends hurt you (through abuse, neglect, betrayal, or some other way), it tends to bring incredible amounts of shame and is very difficult to talk about. You worry that others won't understand. You feel like it's your fault, and you think others might judge you or see you differently. You assume that talking about it will push others further away from you, so you choose to keep it a secret or minimize what's happening. But this secrecy and inauthenticity is actually what's keeping others at a distance.

These experiences of relationship trauma and the resulting outcomes can make it difficult to attempt any connections, even safe and seemingly small ones. To consistently practice making connections, choose someone who feels safe and whom you encounter regularly. Then make small connections with them each time you see them. Choose one of the following examples or create your own. Remember to start with small interactions that feel tolerable (not overwhelming to your nervous system) and slowly build from there.

Say hello each time you see your neighbor

Smile at and make eye contact with your mail carrier

Ask your coworker how their day is going

Give your friend a compliment

Make small talk with the cashier at your local grocery store

Show interest in your classmate's hobbies by asking questions

Thank your partner for small moments (such as doing a chore or listening to you without judgment)

Send your family member a weekly text to let them know you're thinking of them

EXPLORING YOUR RELATIONSHIP FEARS

One common effect trauma has on relationships is deep fear: fear of hurt, abandonment, disappointment, rejection, pain. Here's the thing: Based on your traumatic experiences, these fears are completely understandable. They are also normal. But the depth of these fears is also hurting your relationships by blocking your connections with others. Let's explore how fear might be showing up in your relationships.

1. What are your relationship fears and what are they holding you back from (for instance, from being emotionally or physically intimate, from meeting new people)?

_____

_____

_____

_____

2. What is your biggest relationship fear and what might help you release this fear? (If you're unsure how, you'll find more guidance in the pages ahead.)

_____

_____

_____

_____

3. How do you think your life could improve as you heal and begin to release your relationship fears?

_____

_____

_____

HEALTHY COMMUNICATION IS KEY

Codependency means frequently behaving in a way in which you put others' needs before your own and avoid saying how you really feel, and finding that your mood depends on how someone else is feeling. It often develops in families or close relationships with people who are struggling with substance use, addiction, or mental health. In those kinds of situations, you may have felt pressure to put your own needs aside to avoid conflict, provide support, or "fix" the other person.

Although people who are codependent feel most useful and worthy when they're able to care for another person, they also tend to feel resentful, betrayed, and tired, due to unbalanced relationships where they put in far more energy than they get in return. You might find yourself repeating codependent patterns in your relationships because, although they are painful, these patterns are familiar.

It's not easy to admit to codependent behaviors, and if you recognize them in your relationships, I commend you for taking this brave first step in overcoming these patterns.

One way to heal these patterns and improve your relationships is to learn or relearn healthy communication, and that's the goal of this exercise. Over the course of the next week, choose four of your thoughts that feel important to share (such as how you're feeling, or a need that isn't being met). Write one in each thought bubble, and identify a safe person with whom you'd like to share that thought. Then practice open and direct communication by sharing these thoughts.

I'd like to share this thought with:

_____

I'd like to share this thought with:

_____

I'd like to share this thought with:

_____

I'd like to share this thought with:

_____

WHO YOU SURROUND YOURSELF WITH

Surrounding yourself with safe and supportive people is necessary for healing and growth. The relationships you need now may be different from those you needed in the past, and you might start to recognize some relationships in your life that no longer serve you. You may decide these relationships need new boundaries, less energy given to them, or to be let go of completely.

1. What relationships can you identify in your life that you would like to change, and why?

   _____

   _____

2. How do you think you could improve these relationships? (For example, by expressing your needs, communicating what you feel, or setting better boundaries.)

   _____

   _____

3. What positive qualities do you hope to value and nurture in your relationships in the future that you may not have before?

   _____

   _____

4. Are there any relationships that no longer serve you? Why is that?

   _____

   _____

RELEASING ANGER

Anger is a particularly difficult emotion for many women to feel and express because of deeply ingrained social standards around how women "should" present themselves, which don't include expressing anger. This results in feelings of shame when you feel anger and, ultimately, repress it, to the detriment of your mental and physical health and relationships with others. Anger is like any other emotion, however, and it's important to learn to allow yourself to process it in healthy ways.

Repressing anger and healthy aggression by trying to live up to other people's expectations or being overly nice to win their approval can create difficulties with setting boundaries. This may cause you to become disconnected from your anger or flooded by it, which might lead to you either avoid setting a needed boundary or communicating a boundary in a way that's not well received.

Before communicating a boundary, try using one of the practices listed to physically release the anger you may be feeling toward the situation and help you connect with your anger in a healthy way and communicate your boundary from a more grounded place.

Sit or stand facing the wall, reach your arms straight out, and place your palms flat against the wall (add a pillow between your hands and the wall, if you want). Push into the wall, gradually using more pressure. Then gently release and repeat as needed.

Stomp your feet on the ground.

Punch something soft, like a pillow.

Do the progressive muscle relaxation exercise on page 94.

Let out a scream into a pillow or anywhere private.

Write down your angry feelings, then tear up the piece of paper.

Listen to music that reflects your anger and dance or shake out your feelings using your arms and legs.

MASTERING HEALTHY CONFLICT

Addressing conflict can feel scary and hard, especially if you have codependent or people-pleasing tendencies or had unhealthy models of conflict in your childhood or past relationships. But an important truth to learn is that conflict is a normal part of relationships. Avoiding it can result in repressing your emotions, unresolved conflict festering under the surface of your relationships, and/or cutting people off without attempting to resolve issues in a way that meets your needs (when it's safe to do so). Finding healthy ways to address and resolve conflict is necessary for healthy relationships.

Setting boundaries and getting your needs met are two themes that may arise when addressing conflict, and all three—establishing boundaries, getting your needs met, and addressing conflict in healthy ways—increase safety, trust, and openness in your relationships.

Here are three scenarios in which you'd want to set a boundary, express your needs, and/or address a conflict. For each scenario, fill in the blank with how you'd like to respond.

1. Your friend asks you to go to a party with them this weekend.
   "Instead of that, I'd like to _____
   _____."

2. At a holiday gathering, a family member makes an insensitive comment about your appearance.
   "I'd feel more comfortable if you would/would not _____
   _____
   _____."

3. You and your partner were teasing each other in a lighthearted manner, but your partner doesn't stop when you ask them to.
   "When _____, I feel
   _____. In the future, I'd like if
   you would _____
   _____."

YOUR SUPPORT PEOPLE

In 2022, I got trapped underwater amid powerful Hawaiian waves rolling in and out as I tried to get to shore. It was a scary experience, but my husband's supportive and loving response helped me through it. Instead of being scared to go back in the ocean, I'm able to joke about it with him now (in part because my top came off when I was helped out of the water!). I've been in the ocean many times since, and the experience helped me feel even more safe with and supported by my husband.

I share this as an example of how the support we have (or don't have) during or after a stressful or traumatic experience can make a significant difference in how our minds and bodies respond.

1. When you think about recent challenging or stressful experiences you've had, who were the people (or person) who helped you feel heard, supported, and understood? How did they show these qualities?

_____

_____

_____

_____

_____

2. How do your current healthy relationships contribute to your sense of safety, well-being, and peace?

_____

_____

_____

_____

_____

YOUR HEALING BELIEFS

Following is a list of beliefs you may have when you're operating from a place of hurt in your relationships. With self-reflection on your thoughts, emotions, and behaviors, maybe even the reflection you've done throughout this book, you can raise awareness about how such beliefs might be influencing how you show up in your relationships. This can be a helpful step in healing yourself and your current and future relationships from the effects of trauma.

In the right column, write an example of how each belief of your hurting self has changed for you already or how you hope it will change as you continue on your healing journey.

HURT ME BELIEVES	HEALING ME BELIEVES
When others treat me poorly, it means there's something wrong with me.	*Example: The way others treat me is most often a reflection of them and not of me or my worth.*
If I don't agree with others, they won't like me or want me around.	
Setting boundaries is selfish.	
I have to keep my guard up, because people can't be trusted.	
I need to be in control in order to feel good in my relationships.	
I often judge others and assume that others are judging me.	
Conflict scares me, and I try to avoid it at all costs.	
I'm responsible for others' emotions and their needs are more important than mine.	
Safe and healthy relationships are impossible for me.	

REGULATING TOGETHER

Co-regulation is when you learn to manage your emotions and feel safe by connecting with someone else who helps calm you. One of the first ways you learn to self-regulate your own emotions is through co-regulation. When you are growing up, if your caregivers don't or can't co-regulate with you, you may struggle to navigate and regulate your own emotions and to be open and understanding in your relationships.

As an adult, you can learn to do these things on your own, but co-regulation with another person can still be especially helpful. Through warm interactions with a safe person, you both can become more open to connection and feel more balanced and relaxed.

Choose one person with whom you feel comfortable practicing co-regulation. This may be a romantic partner, a close friend, or a family member. Use the following list to start practicing co-regulation together.

1. Talk in a calm tone.
2. Make gentle eye contact.
3. Touch gently (for example, hold hands or hug).
4. Do activities together that you both enjoy.
5. Practice grounding techniques (page 10) together.
6. Listen to each other without judgment.
7. Spend time together without being on your phones.
8. Sit in a shared space without the pressure of conversation.

LEANING INTO CONNECTION

A positive sign that you're healing is when you seek more connection with safe people and feel less desire to isolate or stay connected with unsafe people. To help assess whether someone is a safe or unsafe person for you, pay attention to your emotional and body cues. For example, with a safe person, you're more likely to feel like you can be yourself with them; while with an unsafe person, you may feel more pressure to be perfect or please them in order to avoid their judgment. When you're around or interacting with a safe person, you might notice that your body feels relaxed, and with an unsafe person, you might experience heightened stress or tension in your body. Use the space provided to explore how you can expand your safe and supportive community.

1. List people with whom you've already connected (such as friends or a significant other) and note how each connection could be improved (perhaps more open communication or more quality time together).

_____

_____

_____

2. Next, list people with whom you'd like to begin building healthy relationships and write about how you might initiate or improve those connections (join a support group, ask a colleague to grab coffee outside of work, or something else).

_____

_____

_____

*As I heal from what hurt me,
I can have the healthy
relationships I desire.*

KEY TAKEAWAYS

Trauma, as well as your early environments, experiences, and attachments, has a deep and lasting impact on relationships. Trauma can show up in your relationships in many ways, such as challenges with fear, trust, setting boundaries, and making yourself vulnerable. It shuts down the social part of the brain, which leads to patterns of disconnection and isolation. As you heal from trauma and surround yourself with safe and supportive people, your relationships will heal, too.

- You can develop secure attachments with safe people, no matter what experiences or attachment wounds you've had in the past.

- You might find yourself repeating codependent patterns in your relationships because, although these patterns are painful, they are familiar.

- The relationships you need now may be different from those you needed in the past, and you might start to recognize some relationships in your life that no longer serve you.

- Co-regulation in a safe relationship can help you navigate and regulate your own emotions and be more open and understanding in your relationships.

- A positive sign that you're healing is when you desire more connection with safe people and feel less desire to isolate or to stay connected with unsafe people.

SECTION 9
RECLAIMING YOUR JOY

You deserve joy. Whether it's feeling the sunshine on your skin, listening to your favorite song, cuddling with your pet, or sharing a blanket on a cold day with someone you love, being able to recognize these moments of joy is healing, and reclaiming joy is a beautiful part of the healing journey. When you start embracing joy, you're able to move out of survival mode and really start to live. You'll be freer to explore and express your authentic self and find acceptance for all parts of you.

Along your healing journey, you'll take steps forward and experience positive moments, have hard days or periods when you feel stuck, and uncover unexpected layers of yourself throughout the process. Understanding the healing process isn't linear gives you permission to show yourself compassion and increases your resilience to make it through the hard days.

While trauma can make life feel stagnant, gloomy, and narrow, healing enables you to broaden and shift your perspective, take back control, and look forward to the future with hope. We'll explore all of this throughout this section, along with handling setbacks and coping with challenges, reaching acceptance, and planning for the future.

"Like the rainbow after the rain, joy will reveal itself after sorrow."

—RUPI KAUR

Jasmine's Story: Blossoming into Post-Traumatic Growth

Jasmine was the only child of a single parent. From the outside looking in, everything appeared okay. But behind closed doors, her parent displayed narcissistic traits and other untreated mental health symptoms. Jasmine received love only when she was doing exactly what was expected of her or when it benefited her parent in some way.

As Jasmine got older and naturally wanted more independence and freedom, she and her parent began having more frequent and intense conflicts, often including belittling comments and Jasmine being blamed for their conflict. Jasmine attempted to escape this pressure and conflict with a very busy schedule outside of school and unhealthy coping skills, such as weekends filled with heavy substance use and risky sexual behavior. She was mostly able to keep it together on the surface, but inside she was struggling painfully.

As an adult, Jasmine started to slowly heal with years of therapy and personal growth work. She used unhealthy coping skills less and less frequently, started to develop deeper and more meaningful relationships, released toxic shame, and embraced her inner child and what brings her joy. She continues to work on self-love and to provide herself with the unconditional love and acceptance that she has never received from her parent.

She had to learn some hard lessons and face challenges along the way, but Jasmine refuses to let her past define her, and she has blossomed into the person she wants to be, living the life she wants to live.

YOUR RESILIENCE IS BEAUTIFUL

You've been through hard things, and your strength has enabled you to persevere and survive. This is proof you are resilient. With this resilience in mind, you can develop a growth mindset; you can flow with life's changes without feeling overwhelmed and grow through both the highs and lows of life, while remembering that growth often happens in moments of discomfort.

Let's take a closer look at the evidence of your resilience. Write a brief description of a challenging situation you've faced. Reflect on it and identify how you have shown resilience to make it through the challenge (for example, you used your coping skills or faced the challenge instead of avoiding it). Then use what you discovered to create two affirmations you can use moving forward to help remind yourself of your resilience (such as *I can face the challenges life throws at me*).

Challenging situation I've faced

_____

How I have shown resilience in the situation

_____

My resilience affirmations

_____

_____

_____

_____

THE TRUTH ABOUT HEALING

When you think about healing trauma, what comes to mind? Sometimes the ideas you have about healing can set up unfair expectations and unintentionally interfere with your healing journey. This quiz explores the truth about healing, to help dispel some common myths. This clearer insight will help you create reasonable expectations and give yourself more grace and understanding along the way.

For the following statements about what healing looks like, circle whether you think they are true or false. Then check your answers at the bottom of the next page.

1. **Absence of all symptoms**
   True   *False*

2. **Managing symptoms becomes easier**
   True   *False*

3. **Decrease in frequency or intensity of symptoms**
   True   *False*

4. **Being well-regulated all the time**
   True   *False*

5. **Being more assertive and setting healthy boundaries**
   True   *False*

6. **Increase in self-compassion**
   True   *False*

7. **Becoming more aware of and connected to your body**
   True   *False*

8. **Drastic and fast progress and growth**
   True   *False*

9. **Helpful shifts in perspective about self, others, and the world**
   True   *False*

10. Learning to process comfortable and uncomfortable emotions

   True   *False*

11. Never getting triggered again

   True   *False*

12. Becoming more open, vulnerable, and present

   True   *False*

13. Seeing the trauma as something that happened to you, not who you are

   True   *False*

14. Constant forward movement with no steps backward

   True   *False*

WHEN YOU FEEL STUCK

At times, you may feel stuck on your healing journey. You may feel as if you've hit a plateau, like you're not making progress or noticing any changes, even though you're putting in the effort to do things differently and to reach your goals. You may feel like resources and skills that were previously helpful are no longer working, or like there's a mental or emotional block getting in the way of being able to further your healing. Or you may even reach a point where you are questioning the purpose of this healing journey you're on and have thoughts about stopping it altogether.

This can be a very normal part of the journey. It might mean a change in your approach to healing could be useful (perhaps try a new skill or technique) or that your nervous system is feeling overwhelmed and you need to slow down or rest. To help prepare for this, use this practice to explore how you plan to address periods when you feel stuck.

1. What are the signs that you're feeling stuck?

   _____

   _____

2. What will you do if you begin to feel stuck on your journey? Are there skills or resources you've found useful in this book or else-where that might help?

   _____

   _____

3. How can you show yourself grace and be patient during these periods?

   _____

   _____

A CALENDAR FOR THE TRUE YOU

"Healing is allowing the worst version of yourself be loved." I read this quote from Lorna Bailey online and fell in love with it. I wholeheartedly believe the goal of healing isn't just to find the so-called best version of yourself, but rather to find acceptance for *all* versions of yourself, even those that are sometimes imperfect, messy, or uncertain or that simply feel uncomfortable to show to others. It's about letting those parts of you that you previously kept hidden and felt ashamed of to be seen and loved by yourself and others. It's about letting those parts be accepted and integrated into the whole you, to give you a sense of completeness and authenticity.

In the coming weeks, use this calendar to take one small step toward acceptance and authenticity each day.

SUN	Forgive yourself for making a mistake.	Find a small way to step outside your comfort zone.
MON	Make one choice that aligns with your values.	Show compassion to a part of you that you feel ashamed of.
TUE	Acknowledge one of your strengths.	Ask someone for help with something you are finding hard.
WED	Celebrate something unique about you.	Treat yourself as you would your close friend.
THU	Notice and name your emotions, either verbally or in writing.	Avoid comparing yourself to anyone else.
FRI	Voice your opinion and speak up for yourself.	Give yourself credit for a recent accomplishment.
SAT	Allow yourself to play, laugh, and be silly.	Open up to a friend about something that's weighing on your mind.

THE EBBS AND FLOWS OF HEALING

Some days you're healing, and other days you're surviving. Some weeks you're struggling, and other weeks you're thriving. None of that is wrong. It's all part of the process. We're meant to go through different seasons as our energy, motivation, mood, and nervous system experiences ebbs and flows. In somatic therapy, these are called *expansions* and *contractions*.

We tend to shame ourselves during times of contraction for not feeling good or productive "enough." Likewise, we can forget to appreciate the moments of positive expansion. To help accept the ebbs and flows as a natural part of your journey, write encouraging, nurturing, or compassionate self-talk you can use during each stage.

The times when I feel excited for the journey:

_____

_____

The times when I feel motivated to do the work:

_____

_____

The times when I feel stuck about what to do next:

_____

_____

The times when I feel overwhelmed by it all:

_____

_____

The times when I feel ready to start again:

_____

_____

EMBRACING OUR WOMANHOOD TOGETHER

Simply being a woman living in this world means you are resilient. Although there have been advances in women's rights, we continue to face cultural challenges that sometimes require us to put in extra effort just to be seen and heard, when being valued should always be available to us. This is one reason it's so important that we look to each other as support rather than competition.

1. Who have been the most influential women in your life?

_____

_____

_____

2. What qualities did they possess that you admire?

_____

_____

_____

3. How can you be more supportive of the women in your life?

_____

_____

_____

4. How can you open yourself up to receive more support from other women?

_____

_____

_____

FINDING JOY EACH DAY

While trauma can cloud your ability to access memories that feel good, those memories are there; they might just need a little more help and patience from you to bring them to awareness. It can feel like nothing good ever happens, especially when you're stressed or overwhelmed, but try not to believe it.

Good things have happened to each and every one of us. Maybe you saw a beautiful sunset at the end of a hard day, had the best cookie ever at your local coffee shop, or laughed until you cried with a good friend. Recognizing these moments and taking time to appreciate them can help increase your sense of presence and feelings of joy in everyday life.

In the coming week, practice noticing and appreciating the little things that bring you joy. Create a keepsake of these moments by writing a few words in the shapes provided describing what brought you joy.

MONDAY

TUESDAY

WEDNESDAY

THURSDAY

FRIDAY

SATURDAY

SUNDAY

REWRITING YOUR STORY

Sometimes it may feel like your past defines who you are and how you see yourself. It's important to know that you can accept and acknowledge the hard things you've been through without taking them on as part of your identity.

For this exercise, recall a time in your life that brings up some challenging or uncomfortable, but tolerable, thoughts or emotions about yourself. Then rewrite your story to take back control and create a new narrative in which you don't feel defined by your past.

The Old Story

1. Describe a challenging chapter in your life.

_____

_____

_____

_____

_____

_____

_____

2. What's the theme of this story (powerlessness, shame, fear, something else)?

_____

3. Give this story a name.

_____

The New Story

1. Choose a new theme for this chapter (perhaps hope, growth, strength, compassion).

   _____

2. Rewrite your story with your new theme in mind.

   _____

   _____

   _____

   _____

   _____

   _____

   _____

   _____

   _____

   _____

   _____

   _____

   _____

   _____

3. Give your new story a new name.

   _____

YOUR CHALLENGES TOOL KIT

You will face challenges along the way; that's a normal part of life and of the healing process. But challenges don't need to derail your healing journey. List up to ten skills and resources you tend to forget when you face a difficulty and feel sad or distressed, such as calling on safe people in your life or using grounding techniques to bring you into the present moment.

1. _____

2. _____

3. _____

4. _____

5. _____

6. _____

7. _____

8. _____

9. _____

10. _____

You can also type your list in your phone or write it somewhere you can easily access when needed (perhaps in a planner or journal, or post it on your bathroom mirror).

FORGIVING YOURSELF

I would never ask you to forgive someone who has hurt you. I believe it can be helpful for healing in some contexts, but not helpful or necessary in others, and that decision is a deeply personal choice you must have full agency in making. I am, however, going to invite you to forgive yourself. Embracing self-forgiveness can guide you toward post-traumatic growth, because it helps change your self-perception and self-beliefs.

1. Make yourself comfortable and bring to mind a situation about which you feel mildly guilty or ashamed.
2. Observe any feelings that come up without judging them as good or bad.
3. Imagine someone you love went through that experience. What would you say to them to offer compassion, acceptance, and forgiveness?
4. Speak these words aloud to yourself.
5. Finish by saying these affirmations to yourself.

I am worthy of forgiveness.

Mistakes are my greatest teachers.

I choose to release shame and embrace self-love.

CRYSTAL BALL THINKING

Have you ever felt like you're behind in life? Like your peers seem to be ahead, achieving more, like they are where you're "supposed" to be? Or maybe you've had a hard time imagining a future life for yourself, or a better future than the life you're experiencing now. If so, you're not alone. These thoughts and beliefs are not uncommon for trauma survivors.

Similarly, there's a thinking error called *crystal ball thinking* that involves focusing on and assuming negative outcomes for your future: *Nothing good will ever happen for me.* To help turn this around, in each image below, write down one positive thing you hope will happen in the next two weeks, month, six months, and year. Include steps you can take to make each vision a reality.

2 WEEKS

1 MONTH

6 MONTHS

1 YEAR

CELEBRATE *ALL* YOUR PROGRESS

You've done an amazing job on your healing journey so far, and I know you'll continue to do so. Throughout your journey, on your good days and the hard ones, you deserve to acknowledge and celebrate your wins. From allowing yourself to rest without guilt, to noticing your triggers, to naming your emotions and using compassionate self-talk, it's important to celebrate your wins, both big and small. As you're celebrating your wins, try not to get caught up in perfectionism or judging yourself. Instead, focus on shifting your perspective and bringing awareness to your progress, even on the hard days. This practice will help you do that.

Find a jar, box, or other small container. Cut out ten to fifteen small pieces of paper, or more if you'd like. On each one, write one way you can celebrate your wins. Then fold the pieces of paper and put them inside your container. Decorate the outside of your container however you'd like. At the end of each week, take time to reflect on and identify one win you'd like to celebrate. Then pick one piece of paper and do the celebration.

Some ideas to celebrate yourself:

1. Give yourself an extra thirty minutes for an activity you enjoy (such as watching TV or reading).
2. Schedule time to do something you've been wanting to do (perhaps go to a museum or see a movie).
3. Treat yourself to a reward (stickers, your favorite drink, or some chocolate).
4. Take a long walk alone or with someone.

HEALING IS LAYERED, LIKE AN ONION

Each section of this book addresses an important area of healing trauma: letting go of shame, exploring emotions, embracing self-care, feeling safe in your body, building self-love, creating healthy relationships, and reclaiming your joy. Each area has many layers to it, and as you process one, another may reveal itself. You'll likely circle back to different layers, and your focus will shift throughout your journey, but having a general idea of your current area of focus can help you set and achieve goals and reduce the possibility of feeling overwhelmed.

1. Which **area has felt the most important to your healing process so far?**

_____

_____

_____

_____

_____

_____

2. Write about one or two areas to focus on now as you continue on your journey. Then set a goal to work on in each area, and list the skills or steps that will help you get there.

_____

_____

_____

_____

_____

_____

I am healing from what happened to me and growing into the person I was meant to be.

KEY TAKEAWAYS

Reclaiming joy includes bringing mindful awareness to joyful moments, embracing your authentic self, taking back control of your life and your self-perceptions, forgiving yourself, and looking forward to the future with hope. Healing does not follow a linear path, and facing challenges or feeling stuck are normal parts of the journey. Understanding the ebbs and flows of a healing journey and having fair expectations for healing help set you up for progress and growth. Remember to give yourself grace on the good days and the hard ones, and celebrate every step of progress along the way.

- You've been through hard things, and your strength enabled you to persevere and survive. This is proof that you are resilient.

- Healing involves allowing all parts of yourself to be seen and loved.

- You don't have to be defined by your past.

- You are not alone on your journey, and travel alongside many other women who share your experiences.

- Embracing self-forgiveness can guide you toward post-traumatic growth as you see yourself in a kinder, more loving light.

A FINAL WORD

You did it! You've reached the end of this book, and I'm so incredibly proud of you. Having walked on this path myself, I can relate to how much effort, reflection, and vulnerability the trauma healing journey asks of you. Take a moment to appreciate all you've done here, and congratulate yourself. Celebrate how far you've come and the beautiful places you're headed.

As you know, healing is an ongoing process, but you're much better equipped to move forward on your healing journey now and to seek further help if you need it. Remember to use the self-compassion skills you've gained to give yourself grace as you continue to heal and restore your sense of self-love.

Also, remember you're not alone. You're not alone in having endured and survived traumatic events, and you're not alone in wanting to heal from the wounds you've experienced. Surround yourself with a safe and supportive community, and don't forget to be the safe and supportive presence you need for yourself, too.

I hope you've found some peace with the understanding that what happened to you was not your fault, and your resulting trauma responses are not wrong or bad; they're extremely adaptive ways your mind and body have protected you from overwhelming stress and pain. I hope that understanding also gives you permission to let go of those responses now. They served a very important purpose, but you don't need them anymore. You've got this now, and you can take it from here.

RESOURCES

Here are a variety of resources you can use to help you continue your journey of healing from trauma.

Apps

SomaShare: An app to help you regulate your nervous system and support healing your body.

Books

Brown, Jordan. *Self-Love Journal for Women*. Emeryville, CA: Callisto, 2023.

Foo, Stephanie. *What My Bones Know*. New York: Ballantine Books, 2022.

Gibson, Lindsay C. *Adult Children of Emotionally Immature Parents*. Oakland, CA: New Harbinger Publications, 2015.

Heller, Diane Poole. *The Power of Attachment*. Louisville, CO: Sounds True, 2019.

Logan, Megan. *Self-Love Workbook for Women*. Emeryville, CA: Callisto, 2020.

Schwartz, Richard. *No Bad Parts*. Louisville, CO: Sounds True, 2021.

Crisis Help

National Eating Disorders Helpline: A 24/7 support line that can offer referrals to treatment options in your area. Call 800-931-2237, text "NEDA" to 741741, or visit nationaleatingdisorders.org/get-help.

988 Suicide & Crisis Lifeline: Find 24/7 assistance if you are feeling depressed or having suicidal thoughts. Call 988 or visit 988lifeline.org.

RAINN: An organization offering 24/7 help for victims of sexual violence. Call 800-656-4673 or visit rainn.org/resources.

Podcasts

The Healing Trauma Podcast, with Monique Koven

The Inner Child Podcast, with Gloria Zhang

Trauma Rewired Podcast, with Jennifer Wallace and Elisabeth Kristof

The Trauma Therapist Podcast, with Guy Macpherson

Therapist Directories

Art Therapy: arttherapy.org
/art-therapist-locator

Brainspotting Therapy:
brainspotting.com/directory

EMDR Therapy: emdria.org
/find-an-emdr-therapist

Equine Therapy: pathintl.org
/find-a-program

Individual and Group Therapy:
psychologytoday.com

International Therapy:
internationaltherapistdirectory.com

Reduced Fee Therapy:
openpathcollective.org

Substance Use Therapy:
findtreatment.gov

Websites

Natewrites.com: Find free resources,
including inner child journaling and
an extensive resource guide
on trauma

Self-compassion.org: Find information
about and guided practices for
self-compassion

REFERENCES

Boulder Valley Care Network. "10 Trauma Sensitive Yoga Poses." mybvcn.org/documents/10-trauma -sensitive-yoga-poses.pdf. Accessed September 10, 2024.

Brach, Tara. *Radical Acceptance: Embracing Your Life with the Heart of a Buddha*. New York: Viking, 2004.

Buczynski, Ruth, et al. "Working with Core Beliefs of 'Never Good Enough.'" National Institute for the Clinical Application of Behavioral Medicine. nicabm.com/confirm /never-good-enough/.

Dana, Deb. *Polyvagal Card Deck*. New York: W. W. Norton & Company, 2022.

Edwards, Steph [@toyoufromsteph]. "You can't do it all at once. One day at a time my lovely." Instagram, 9 December. 2024, instagram.com/p/DDXOih5in17.

Foo, Stephanie. *What My Bones Know: A Memoir of Healing from Complex Trauma*. New York: Ballantine Books, 2022.

Hofmann, Stefan, et al. "Loving Kindness and Compassion Meditation: Potential for Psychological Interventions." *Clinical Psychology Review*. 2011. sciencedirect.com /science/article/abs/pii /S0272735811001115?via%3Dihub.

Kaur, Rupi. *The Sun and Her Flowers*. Kansas City, MO: Andrews McMeel Publishing, 2017.

Kearney, David, et al. "Loving-Kindness Meditation for Posttraumatic Stress Disorder: A Pilot Study." *Journal of Traumatic Stress*, U.S. National Library of Medicine, July 25, 2013. pubmed.ncbi.nlm.nih.gov/23893519/.

Levine, Peter. *Healing Trauma*. Louisville, CO: Sounds True, 2008.

Marlow-MaCoy, Amy, and Amy Kempe. *The Clinician's Guide to Treating Adult Children of Narcissists*. Eau Claire, WI: PESI Publishing, Inc., 2023.

Maté, Gabor. *The Myth of Normal: Trauma, Illness and Healing in a Toxic Culture*. New York: Avery, 2022.

Menakem, Resmaa. *My Grandmother's Hands: Racialized Trauma and the Pathway to Mending Our Hearts and Bodies*. Las Vegas, NV: Central Recovery Press, 2017.

Perry, Bruce, and Oprah Winfrey. *What Happened to You?: Conversations on Trauma, Resilience*, and Healing. New York: Flatiron Books, 2021.

Schwartz, Arielle. *A Practical Guide to Complex PTSD: Compassionate Strategies to Begin Healing from Childhood Trauma*. Emeryville, CA: Callisto, 2020.

Schwartz, Arielle. *The Complex PTSD Workbook: A Mind-Body Approach to Regaining Emotional Control & Becoming Whole*. Berkeley, CA: Althea Press, 2016.

Siegel, Daniel J. *Mindset: The New Science of Personal Transformation*. New York: Viking, 2010.

Sigurdardottir, Sigrun, et al. "Consequences of childhood sexual abuse for health and well-being: Gender similarities and differences." *Scandinavian Journal of Public Health*. 2014; 42:278–286. doi: 10.1177/1403494813514645.

Sincero, Jen. *You Are a Badass: How to Stop Doubting Your Greatness and Start Living an Awesome Life*. Philadelphia, PA: Running Press, 2013.

Sweeton, Jennifer. *Trama Treatment Toolbox*. Eau Claire, WI: PESI Publishing, Inc., 2019.

Vogt, Dawne. "Research on Women, Trauma and PTSD." U.S. Department of Veterans Affairs, ptsd.va.gov/professional/treat/specific/ptsd_research_women.asp. Accessed September 10, 2024.

INDEX

emotions (*continued*)

    of, 49, 56

    expectations for, 57

    feeling, 49, 65

    glimmer journaling, 64

    grief, 69

    healing past, 55, 71

    impact of trauma
on, 48, 71

    mindfulness exer-
cises for, 68

    naming, 50–51

    needs and, 79–80

    nervous system
and, 61–63

    playlists for, 66–67

    RAIN exercise, 60

    safe spaces for, 58–59

expansions, 154

F

family, 3, 129

fight, flight, freeze, or fawn
response, 4, 15, 22–23,
66–67, 76, 96

Foo, Stephanie, 17

friendships, 3

G

gender roles, traditional, 7

glimmers, 64

gratitude, 106

grief, 69

grounding techniques, 10,
58–59, 93

growth mindset, 26, 149

guilt, 90

H

healing

    beliefs, 142

    calendar for, 153

    challenges to, 25–26

    as a journey, 15

    layers of, 164

    paths to, 23–24, 27

    possibility of, 13

    readiness for, 18

    safety and, 19–20, 24, 27

    seasons of, 154–155

    tips for, 20–23, 24–25

    truth about, 150–151

Heller, Diane Poole, 133

help, asking for, 23

hyperarousal, 61–62

hypervigilance, 5, 7, 15

hypoarousal, 61–62

I

identity confusion, 3

imperfectionism, 41

inner child

    comforting, 38

    letter to, 83

    visualizing, 81

Internal Family Systems
(IFS) therapy, 114–116

J

joy, 147, 157, 166

K

Kaur, Rupi, 148

L

letter writing

    to inner child, 83

    to release shame, 45

    to your body, 106

LGBTQ+ people, 3

loss, 69

loving-kindness
meditation, 113

M

Maté, Gabor, 3, 48

media consumption, 85

memories, 98–99

Menakem, Resmaa, 90

mental health conditions,
trauma and, 9

mind-body adaptations, 4,
5–6, 12, 15, 25, 98

mindful imagery, 68, 116

mindful movement, 10, 105

mindfulness exercises

    for experiencing emo-
tions, 68

    for feeling over-

recovering from, 13, 15
responses to, 5–6, 25
symptoms, 7–9
unresolved, 19
women and, 6–7, 52

U

unhealthy coping strate-
gies, 5–6, 15, 74,
88, 90, 148
unresolved trauma, 19

V

values, 123
vulnerability, 24, 39

W

window of tolerance,
61–63, 66–67, 71
womanhood,
embracing, 156
women, trauma
and, 6–7, 52

Y

yoga, 105

ACKNOWLEDGMENTS

For everyone who is healing from trauma, whether you're taking your very first step or are years into your journey, I see you and admire your incredible strength and courage.

And for my husband—thank you for fully loving and accepting me and for being the truest friend I've ever had.

ABOUT THE AUTHOR

Jordan Brown, MS, LPC, specializes in helping young women navigate challenging relationships with parents, overcome overwhelming perfectionism and people-pleasing, and heal from complex trauma. She owns a Wisconsin-based mental health group practice and uses compassion-focused, cognitive, and somatic approaches in her work. She is passionate about helping her clients see and believe in their worth, treat themselves with all the kindness and care they deserve, and find meaningful connection with others.

Outside of the office, you'll find Jordan spending time with her husband and their two cats, Diggle and Pepper, being active, and traveling. (She hopes to see all of the Caribbean and every U.S. national park.)